VAYAM SATVERSE

Aumnism
THE FIRST RAY OF DAWN
PART 1

SHYAMIVA AND SWAPNIL ARORA

© Shyamiva and Swapnil Arora 2023

All rights reserved

All rights reserved by author. No part of this publication may be reproduced, stored in a retrieval system or transmitted in any form or by any means, electronic, mechanical, photocopying, recording or otherwise, without the prior permission of the author.

Although every precaution has been taken to verify the accuracy of the information contained herein, the author and publisher assume no responsibility for any errors or omissions. No liability is assumed for damages that may result from the use of information contained within.

First Published in February 2023

ISBN: 978-93-5704-960-3

BLUEROSE PUBLISHERS
www.BlueRoseONE.com
info@bluerosepublishers.com
+91 8882 898 898

Cover Design:
Pooja Bishnoi

Typographic Design:
Pooja Sharma

Distributed by: BlueRose, Amazon, Flipkart

Dedicating this book to the most beautiful angels

~~~Tiana and Parisha~~~

About Swapnil

Swapnil hails from the stunning city of Udaipur, surrounded by picturesque lakes. Trained as a Chartered Accountant, he currently serves at a Public Sector Bank, yet his true passion lies in writing. A bilingual scribe, he now resides in Bhopal and has been inspired by spirituality to pursue his writing dreams.

Through his work, he endeavors to bring positivity and love to humanity by blending the power of spiritualism into his words. He hopes to reach the hearts and souls of readers, connecting with them on a profound level. To Swapnil, if even one person's life is positively impacted by his writing, he will consider his mission accomplished.

Swapnil can be connected here:

- www.swapnilarora.in
- swapnilarora@outlook.com
- www.instagram.com/vayamsatverse
- www.youtube.com/@vayamsatverse

Additionally, one can dive into spirituality with him at www.yogbhakti.me

A Note From Shyamiva

When this book was started, the only intent has been, to be able to help humanity at large by passing over the knowledge of the spiritual experiences we had in our journey. We are just the medium of the divine guidance that is strongly needed in present time of changing yugas. With the world in distress, hope Aumnism is like that ray of sunshine in lives of all of you. May you all find your true selves and become one with the pure love of almighty. Lots of love and blessings.

HARI OM TAT SAT

Preface

Per aspera ad astra

(Through hardships to the stars)

We think the journey of a soul starts from childhood but maybe it all starts much before. Does it commence from previous birth's action and effect, or does it start even before we take human avatar, maybe since the moment the souls were stimulated into creation. Is it all destined by some higher power above, and we are mere puppets, or are we creators of our own journey? Is it, in moments of pure awareness as souls, we choose our own life paths and circumstances and have the power to rise above to change our timelines, or we adopt a shortcut to escape and blame it all on destiny? We often juggle with these questions, fun part, mostly when we face adverse circumstances and darkness around us. Then sometimes we ponder who am I? Where am I going? What do I want? Am I following my soul's voice or mere a victim of own mind made prison. If it is all cheery merry in life, perfect childhood, perfect youth, perfect marriage, no challenges then will we not be mere homo sapiens with minimum use of our mental capacity. That is why, on earth, there is no concept of perfectness, it is more about embracing our flaws with open arms and transforming it to higher frequency. The beauty that is there in falling, learning, and then walking just like a kid, won't be there if we all came with downloaded programme to live perfectly. Perhaps, that is where robots were invented.

However, if we become mere observers and aware, we can understand this complex matrix of our thoughts, actions, reactions, emotions and their triggers. Everything is then perceived as a stage play or like a canvas where we are the actors and painters of our own canvas, which is part of a 'leela". Though the awakening in real means happens after dark night of a soul, and all those on the path of this journey can relate to it.

This is a story of one such soul, who met other souls in the journey, and his dance, his voyage from ast (illusion) to sat (truth) and everything in between. The fragments of his present birth were woven up above in another dimension by his spirit with threads of previous carnations on earth so that his current one can be the platform for next step to the ladder of evolution for his way back to his true home.

"Are you ready Avalokit?" echoed a male voice in huge circular white dome with projector like screen in panorama style covering the entire interior of dome walls.

"Yes, I guess I am, or I have to be, do we have another option?" he was not very elated doing this all over again, but he understood as he stood in the middle of the panorama theatre. He was in his spirit world!

"Okay, so we will show you glimpses of different timelines with the spirits you have already chosen as your family, friends and loved ones. Now, choose the best possible scenario that will help you to overcome your past birth patterns of same emotional blocks and choices based upon from your past human lives. As you know this will be very important birth in your soul journey because of huge transformational shift happening on earth for the new yuga, make sure to make most use of it. We are here to assist and guide you," A very calm and loving voice echoed again.

"Yes, I understand. I wish to choose a difficult birth, at emotional level, and want to choose such circumstances that will really push me this time to rise above my old embedded emotional and mental threads along with karmic seeds. I am ready this time more than ever. I know this is going to be extremely hard and lonely life, full of emotional turmoil like a roller coaster ride. I will have to encounter duality in emotions, manipulations, and control by family followed by expectations of versions out of me as per choices, opposite to what my core is. I also understand they will be just a medium for me to learn my lessons and in actual helping me to be a better version of my own self by pushing me against the waters. I will try this time to break the chains of attachments and shackles of blocks. I am willing to do whatever it takes this time to make this my last birth!", he said with great will power and determination.

"We are pleased to see your determination, if you are really choosing this timeline, then you will receive help from a very special and divine soul who will act as a catalyst to amplify your journey to another level, so make sure to add various universal signs, symbols while creating your timeline that keep reminding you of your mission and not to miss this golden opportunity. Remember, if you choose up to be in the same past mind patterns and cages even after the help, the future timeline of your birth will change and shape accordingly, and that part is still a mystery and won't be visible as of now in this view" echoed the voice again. "Our choices on earth carve the pave for us and change our predestined timelines."

"I am aware. I think I am ready now and so are my current chosen life mates, time for me to go, goodbye will meet you again. Lots of love!" he said.

"Good luck, Avalokit, may your name in this life will be same as your higher self-name, that is a blessing we bestow upon you so that you are reminded whenever you get lost in your life path."

Contents

Chapter 1: Childhood 1

Chapter 2: Dehradun Diaries 13

Chapter 3: Taravi 18

Chapter 4: Sans Tara 58

Chapter 5: Marriage 80

Chapter 6: Gauri 107

Chapter 7: The Foundation 124

Chapter 8: Dark And Light 141

Chapter 9: Pearls Of Gauri 174

Chapter 10: The Tunnel 214

~~~As you start to walk on the way, **the way appears** – Rumi~~~

Chapter 1

Childhood

A soul descendent down to Earth,

It is time to learn and become what you are worth,

For opportunities and lessons, there is no dearth,

Evolve, to end the cycles of death and Birth!

As the blessings from above, his maternal aunt, Nandita Aunty, gave Avi's name as everyone used to call her. Nandita Aunty, along with her nuclear family of four, was settled in Thiruvananthapuram (aka Trivandrum) since some time. Both, she, and her husband were into IT and were working in a major software giant MNC there.

Before his birth, she had developed her interest into Buddhism lately and had been studying a lot about the sect and been going to many Buddhist places off late. It all started with a family trip to Tibet, their first in like after 6 years, where she had got mesmerised with the silence, the serene and pristine rivers, the climate, the flora, culture, Tibetan art, their food, the music, everything. The culture just mesmerised her to the core and she fell in love with it. Something connected the cord with her soul. Moreover, after that, there was like no turning back. She started following the Buddhist practices and knowing about their culture and went to many places like Sanchi stupas near Bhopal,

Madhya Pradesh, Bodh Gaya in Bihar, Sarnath near Kashi, or Varanasi, where Budhha first gave his teachings of 'Dharma'. She had a recent visit to 'Agasthiyar Mountains' or the 'Pothigai' in a camping trip. It is a sacred place, both in Hindu and Buddhist traditions, where it is believed that Sage Agastya learnt Tamil in 'Mount Potalaka' from "Avalokitesvara' who is a bodhisattva[1], known for his eternal compassion.

Avalokitesvara, the embodiment of boundless compassion and mercy, is revered as the bodhisattva[1] who embodies the compassion of all Buddhas. It is said that he vowed to postpone his own enlightenment until he had helped every sentient being on earth achieve liberation from suffering and the cycle of birth and death.

According to legend, his deep grief at the suffering of others caused his head to split in two, and it was from this tear that his consort, the goddess Tara, was born. Some believe that Tara emerged from a lake created by the tear, while others say she emerged from Avalokitesvara's heart. Hindus and Buddhists alike worship Avalokitesvara, who is also seen as a manifestation of Lord Shiva.

On the eve of Avi's birth, Nandita Aunty dreamed of Avalokitesvara, whose radiant white body and loving expression exuded calm and compassion. His hands moved in sacred mudras as he smiled serenely, seeming to bless Nandita with a love that penetrated the very soul.

When she went on to see Avi after he was born, she immediately felt a lot of love and compassion, as if coming from him. She got tears in her eyes, seeing him, and as if the dream of Avalokitesvara, his compassion, his smile, his

---

[1] A person walking the path of salvation or becoming 'Buddha'

calm, and the present, synced properly. The feeling, the love, that compassion, was strikingly similar. With tears in her eyes, she started murmuring, 'Ava..., Av....' but had lumps in her throat and could not complete the name. All she could manage to say at the end was, Avi! And that is how Avi got his name as a shortened version of Avalokitesvara.

Avi was quite a gifted child since childhood, as a toddler, he used to see many spirits around him. He was five years old, and his maternal grandmother had recently passed away. One day, he was playing with his toys, and he saw her spirit smiling at him and blessing him. He told his mom, "See, granny has come to say bye to you", he chirped excitedly pointing towards her.

"What are you saying, Avi? You must be imagining, daydreaming. Kids nowadays say anything! Or are you making any fun here? Listen Avi don't do this ever again! I don't like these kinds of jokes. Ever, and mind you ever, if you spoke like this again, you will find me in my worst of moods" she brushed him off. Parents often don't believe their children because of their own conditioning. It is said that kids are very open and have psychic visions till five years of age, then, slowly, it diminishes, if parents don't believe them or flourish it. Even as a child, he was renowned for his tender heart and compassionate nature. The smallest hint of suffering could bring tears to his eyes, and he could not bear to see others in pain, no matter how they had treated him. His sensitivity and empathy were his defining traits, and he wore them like a mantle, always ready to offer comfort and understanding to those in need.

Avi had difficult time adjusting to school. He, with his gifts, could not often relate to the education system of mugging everything and pouring in exams and accordingly a child used to be graded and judged. He was good in maths and science but couldn't do social studies where he had to mug up with no logical reasoning and used to flunk. His parents at home couldn't understand this and often used to scold and compare him with his peers.

"Avi why are these marks in social studies so low? Do we give so many fees in school to see this result? Look at your friend Aman's result, that boy excels in every paper. His mother always brags about him whenever we have kitty parties. I, at times, hate going there because of you. I wish I could have a son like Aman, huh" His mother used to scold him very critically.

"This is not what we expect from you Avi, we want you to excel in each and every sphere and make us proud in society," his father's cold and unemotional words used to pierce little Avi's, sensitive heart. Although he was not one to stand up for himself or let others' teasing get to him, he couldn't help being who he was - a deeply emotional and sensitive person. He longed for his parents to understand and accept this about him and would often retreat to his bedroom to cry after enduring their critiques and lack of understanding. He wished they would ask him lovingly about his struggles and offer to help, rather than constantly pushing him to be something he wasn't. All he wanted was love and understanding, and he would have gone to great lengths to earn it, but all he received was the opposite. He had forgotten that he had chosen this in his past life, so as not to succumb to the self-absorbed behaviour of his parents. Little did they realize that their own unresolved issues were causing Avi's emotional foundation to become distorted and blocked, impacting his life in ways they could never have imagined.

His parents loved him, in their own way. But they were unaware of his abilities, his gifts, his sensitivity, his compassion, his free-flowing love for everyone and everything around. Their love was conditioned in accordance with the society. It started becoming childhood scars or traumas, which made him go inwards. As he was not able to express himself that freely, as the society always had something or the other for him. He was imposed restrictions, boundaries, which he did not like, tried to revolt, but was silenced.

Parents use lots of resorts at times, so that their child behave the way they want, in the society. Their societal image and all become so important, that anything else cease to matter as it becomes their obsession in a way. Unknowingly, because of these boundaries, these tactics, they create blocks around their child, and it really hits hard, especially, to children like Avi who are sensitive.

A child will always be a child, if, he is allowed to remain a child, while he is a child.

From a young age, Avi possessed a highly developed empathic gift, which allowed him to sense the mental health of his classmates. He could feel their anxiety, depression, speech difficulties, stammering, feelings of being unloved or left out, lack of joy or happiness in any situation, sadistic outlook on life, introversion, and lack of confidence. He tried to offer them support and care, but they often pushed him away, as many of them were bullies. As he had no one to share his experiences with and was often mistreated at home and school, he began to close off his gift and his heart, building a wall around himself as a defense mechanism. This marked the beginning of the deeply embedded scars within him and the loss of a part of himself. He lived in a sort of delusion, where everything seemed just and right.

In addition to this, the constant chaos at home between his parents led them to take out their frustrations and anger on him, blaming him for their own petty issues. They were unaware of the negative energy they were directing towards him. A child's energy is like a sponge, absorbing whatever is reflected at home, whether it be the silent thoughts, mood swings, aggression, or addictions of the parents, or the love, compassion, and understanding. Avi had already closed himself off and lowered his energy, and with each additional outburst of negative energy at home, he began to suffer from frequent illnesses such as fever, colds, coughs, headaches, and insomnia at a young age. The constant negativity and lack of support at home took a toll on his physical and emotional well-being, and he struggled to maintain his sense of self and happiness.

Avi was slowly becoming like a dumping bin, without any outlet he started to grow more inwards, introvert, silent, less confident and stopped taking stands even when it is the question of life and death. The avoidance and wall in him were becoming a tool to supress, impacting extremely his physical, emotional, and mental growth to an extent that he started to have suicidal tendencies in his childhood itself!

He stopped feeling any love for himself. He had no self-worth, whatsoever. He started seeing himself as a failure in society as he started seeing himself a misfit. He could not gather the confidence to do things which his friends could do in like fraction of seconds. It was due to the control his parents and other people around had imposed on him since his childhood. Parents, at times, when see their child doing something or exuding something which is not in terms with the society, tries to 'control' this considering it to 'erratic' not understanding that every child is different. Novak Djokovik once said, "Building a solid foundation in the early years of child's life will not only help him or her reach their full potential but will also result in better societies as a whole." It is imperative to understand each child, the way they are and not the way, we are, as society. Perhaps, parents need to heal themselves first before giving birth a child, so that children don't have to heal from them.

It was in his senior secondary years some comfort came in his life as he made two close friends, but he couldn't be true version of himself with them because till then he had supressed and congested himself a lot. He masked it by creating a new personality of himself, a happy-go-lucky type, joking all around, jolly, laughing at the surface level and just living life as it is like a nomad not giving much thought about anyone and anything. No one could tell by looking at him what is inside him, the deepest of scars he managed to hide very well. His two friends understood him a bit but gave him his space.

The school was over, Avi somehow moved on in his life. He wanted to pursue his career in either music or other sort of fine arts, but it was bluntly turned down by his parents.

"No Avi! Have you lost your mind, there is no career in all this bizarre stuff, what will people say our son couldn't even secure a decent job?" they said sternly.

"But I won't do it by my heart, I never asked anything please, let me pursue what I like" he pleaded.

"Life is not lived with heart Avi, but with money. We are your parents! We know what is best for you. At your age we also had dreamt of becoming something. This age is such when we think we can do anything. We can aim for stars, but that is not practical, not real. Stay grounded. Don't get fooled by seeing some people doing well in music or arts. Not everyone is that lucky or has that kind of contact in that industry. We are simple people, with simple means. Come to terms with it or you could have taken birth in those families then. Why did you take birth here?" they used to snap at him.

He was so devastated as his dreams came crashing down, he knew parents are not wrong always. Their advice and opinions matter a lot. However, it is important to listen and understand what their child thinks, wants, and feels, as well. He used to take advice from his besties about this, one specially he would never forget "I think Avi, as a parent, it is important to understand the needs and feelings of a child and suggest and advice accordingly and not as per the bias or spectacles of the society. Not to make the child a version, we as a parent want to project to the society. We need to accept children as they are. Every child is different and important. If we need Doctors, Engineers, Accountants, Entrepreneurs, etc., then we also need Singers, Poets, Musicians, Travellers, Healers, Painters, Politicians, Economists, and so on. There is nothing right or wrong in any profession, any job, anything. But in process of making our child 'something', let us not kill the core or the foundation of his journey as a human being. Before schooling a kid, parents need schooling too! And the society, well, it will never be happy, come what may! Even if a child scores a 99, they will be like, "See, could not score a perfect score!". Will there ever be a totally happy and a perfect society? Never! So let us not fall into the false premises of it. A song that totally resonate with this, *"Society you are a crazy breed, I hope you are not lonely without me"* by Eddie Vedder." His bestie often used to hum it. Avi knew he is going against his inner voice but with a shattered and heavy heart, he went to Mumbai for his higher studies and got admission to a decent college, as per the wishes of his parents.

It was like entering a new phase of life, which it truly was. He met new people and encountered different mindsets in the bustling metropolis. At first, he struggled to adapt to the culture shock of moving from a small town to Mumbai. However, he eventually came to appreciate all that the city had to offer.

Mumbai is one of the most populous city in India, the financial capital of the nation as it is called. Also known as 'Maya Nagri', as it is city of opportunities and dreams. Indian Film Industry, 'Bollywood' flourishes within the realms of the city. The city has derived its name from 'Mumba Devi' the deity of local community. The city has been a favourite to every invader of India as once, it was the gateway to enter India from sea routes.

It is a conglomeration of different cultures. A lot of people from various parts of the country flock in for better employment opportunities, business, and education. The city is always busy due to such varied business and employment cultures. That is why it is said that Mumbai never sleeps.

Eventually, he came to embrace the chaos of this new city. Despite the challenges, he found this new life to be invigorating and refreshing. He quickly adapted to the Marathi culture, even going so far as to speak the language fluently, and developed a fondness for vada pav, a local snack that soon replaced his beloved samosas. He revelled in the independence he found here, relishing the opportunity to make his own decisions about where to invest his money and how to spend his time. All of this helped him grow more confident and self-assured. Talking to different mindset people too. His blocks were slowly receding as he was opening again, taking his own decisions, growing outwards again. In his college he was crazily infatuated with a girl, his very first love but he couldn't express his feelings to her. They were very good friends. They used to bunk classes, chat day and night, took long strolls at marine drive. She used to share about her everything and anything, but Avi had a hard time opening there. During their graduation ceremony day, they both went near beach in evening, and as they were silently watching the sunset she asked him, "Avi, we have been friends together for two years now. The college is about to get over. You never shared anything deeply about yourself, did you? It seems like do I even know you?".

"There is nothing to share much about me. But yeah, one thing, I love spending time with you. The college life had not been the same without you. In this new city, new place, new life, you have been an important anchor in my life here. Our chats, our doing all those funny and nasty stuff together, were really like my lifeline. Your taking care of me, making poha for me on some days, all of it meant a lot to me. I don't speak much, but I do feel. I am a little shy at expressing things but have lot of things inside of me" he said with lot of affection looking in her eyes.

"Tell me something I don't know. Is there something you want to tell me?" she persisted.

"I like you!" Finally, he blurted out.

"Avi, I've been waiting for you to say this for two years. I always had a feeling, but I couldn't be sure because you never said it - not even a hint. Why, Avi? You know, I liked you too. I waited and waited for you to make a move, but you never did. There was just something that didn't feel right between us, like something wasn't clicking. You were always so closed off, like you were hiding from me. I felt like you weren't even sure about me, and that's why you never expressed your feelings. And then, three months ago, someone else proposed to me. He told me how I was the center of his universe and poured out his feelings for me. It took me some time, but I finally said yes. You know why? Because I know how it feels to not be chosen. He loves me a lot, even if it's not as pure as it could have been with you. But if you don't understand the magic of your own love, how can anyone else? I just wanted to know what you've been feeling about me all this time. I thought our connection deserved that much, and I guess it's time for closure. I'm not angry with you, just a little sad that our connection couldn't turn into something more beautiful. But as they say, it's all destined. Maybe that's all our destiny had in store for us. I wish you the best of luck. Do you have anything to say before I go?" She spoke with a hint of disappointment, but also with understanding.

Avi's throat choked, he couldn't say anything apart from "Good luck, I hope you get all the happiness in your life. Happy to know that you found love. I will miss you, certainly." and that's how his own wounds, caused his first heartbreak as well. She walked away while he was still sitting on the beach, staring at the waves crashing the shore, it was almost night. He did not shed a tear because he knew about the web he was stuck in; he was just feeling numb. His mind was doing all the talking, "I know I am stuck in my wounds and scars, and no one cares about it".

"Should I go deep inside this sea to feel how it is to be without pains. Am I that valueless to deserve all the pains and suffering, why what have I done? Why the life is so unfair to me. Is there even any GOD up there?"

Suddenly, it was as if a voice spoke to him from within, saying, "Don't lose faith, my dear. You attract what you think and focus on constantly. Take control of your life and choose yourself and unconditional love, for you deserve nothing less. Do this with conviction and watch the magic unfold. A whole new world is waiting for you, like old petals falling away to make room for new growth."

Something like stirred inside him, like a divine intervention. He always thought of others first and kept choosing them, marring his own wishes, joy and here is he now, in this pitiful state. It is no one else's fault but his own, for never choosing his own self and putting blame on everyone else and his own destiny. He cannot live in this victim web of his mind anymore. No one can force anyone anything if we ourselves are strong enough to listen to our own soul voice, as we cannot make anyone happy in life even if we do our best. There has to be a line, a limit, and he felt a sudden upsurge of power inside him.

He looked up at the twinkling stars above and, with a deep sense of determination, silently declared, "This is my life and no one else's." Closing his eyes, he opened his soul, spirit, and every cell of his body to the universe, silently requesting its magic and guidance. As he walked home that evening, he couldn't shake the feeling that something miraculous was about to happen. Everywhere he looked, he saw the number 111 - a sign he couldn't quite decipher, but one that filled him with a sense of intuition and hope.

Chapter 2

Dehradun Diaries

> Where everything is still,
> And the heart flow!!
> Amidst the towering silence,
> Just the sound of heart beats grow!

Dehradun! Not just the place but somehow the name itself strikes a chord inside your heart. The name itself fills you up with love as if some person who has long been to a desert has seen a downpour, which may be similar to the weather of this place. There is love in every atom of this place which percolates down to you when you are there. There are different kinds of cities, some which don't sleep, some which are silent like anything, then there is this place which has beauty & stillness of mountains, music of water & rivers, coolness to the eyes of its flora, and adrenaline rush of the crowd. It's a beautiful combination of new and old; Stillness and movement; the poise of backward, pause and forward. It is an amalgamation of old traditions and culture with contemporary values. This place has a vibe, one probably can never find anywhere else. This city, this beautiful city, grows on you!

Dehradun's name is a combination of two words as per the folklore namely, Dehra (Read Dera) and Dun. It is believed that Sikh Guru (s) had made their base at this place, which means "Dera" and Dun means valley, a base in a valley, meaning thereby. There are, though, other interpretations as well which link the name to the Mahabharata era.

Dehradun, most often also called as Doon Valley, is on the foothills of the Himalayas. Year-round the climate remains mild with good thunderstorms and rains throughout the year. The temperature in winter go very cold as the city is placed on the foothills of the Himalayan Range. And since there is a considerable difference in elevation at various places, the difference in temperature is normal within the radius of city itself. But overall, the temperature remains beautiful and romantic.

The cosmos had plans for Avi, as it has for everyone, though he was unaware of them. After completing of his MBA, he landed a job in a corporate and eureka, he got his posting at Dehradun. There is always a reason for whatever happening around us. We fail to see the bigger picture at times though.

Avi was enjoying his stay at Dehradun. The charm of the city allowed his heart to flow in its high potential. Robbers Cave (Guchhu Paani) gave him the experience of a lifetime. A beautiful long cave filled with waist-high chilled waters. At the end of the cave, that small gush and pool of water make it even more beautiful. The serenity in the place, even in between so much noise, made this place his most beaten path. And to eat Maggi noodles with a cup of tea in those shallow waters at the entrance of cave used to make it a much more complete experience. It felt as if this place drenched his soul in abundance with love, calmness, completeness and oneness with nature and everyone around. He felt elated here. The cool of this place, the feel around and sound of those waters makes him go in almost a trance like state.

Nearby, the Tapkeshwar Temple - a Shiva temple, was another favourite spot for Avi. He had always been a devotee of Shiva, feeling the god's presence around him since childhood. He found comfort in looking at pictures of Shiva, participating in his Aarti ceremonies, gazing at statues of the deity and Shiva Linga, and simply hearing the name "Shiva." The temple held a special place in Avi's heart, and he often found himself drawn to its peaceful atmosphere.

His picture always had his eyes half shut with a third eye located at the centre of his forehead. It always used to give Avi so much calm and serenity, that he himself at times used to feel mild trance state. Shiva is considered to be Adi Yogi, the first Yogi of the cosmos. He is also considered to be creator of Universe along with Shakti. Shiva is considered to be the manifestation of divine masculine energies of the cosmos and shakti to be feminine. There can be no Shiva without Shakti and no Shakti without Shiva. It is said that they both reside inside each and every one of us. The shakti's abode is at Mooladhara (Root Chakra) and Shiva's abode is considered to be at Ajna (Third eye Chakra). Shiva is related to consciousness and Shakti to Energy. When energy and consciousness start interacting with each other, they indulge in cosmic play (leela) which paves its way for creation. This divine and cosmic play keeps on going and after the end of every age, the same gets dissolved in its own. Without consciousness and energy (Shiva and Shakti), no life form can sustain. Consciousness is the state of being aware, to bear knowledge, while energy is becoming, engaging, flowing, manifestation through motion.

Avi felt an indescribable sense of awe at Tapkeshwar Temple. Some wonders of nature can only be experienced, and this was certainly one of them. As he entered the temple, he felt his thoughts begin to quiet, as if each cell of his body was dissolving and transporting him to another realm. The Shiva Linga, a vertical oval-shaped stone symbolizing Shiva, was located inside a cave where water from an unknown source continuously poured over it. It was a Swayambhu Linga, one that had appeared on its own rather than being crafted by humans. A stream flowed between the Shiva Linga cave and several smaller shrines within the temple grounds on the opposite side. One of these shrines contained a human-sized statue of Shiva seated inside a small cave. Avi loved to sit in front of this statue, feeling the vibrant energies within the cave and entering a trance-like, meditative state. It was as if Shiva himself was present in that space. As Avi closed his eyes and sat in front of the statue, he felt energies racing through his body, as if some sort of healing was taking place. These moments of trance were something truly special.

He was in complete awe of this city, Dehra Dun. The long rides on Rajpur road and Mussoorie road. Yummilicious Thai or Tibetan food at "Orchard Restaurant" with amazing views of Himalayan foothills. The peace and serenity of Gurudwara Paonta Sahib which was just an hour's drive far from the city. The list is everlasting.

One day at the office, Avi's colleague Ajeet approached him. "Hey Avi, have you heard about this three-day camping tour at Mussoorie and Chakrata?" Avi had been to Mussoorie before and had always been drawn to the scenic hill station, affectionately known as the "Queen of Hills." But he had an additional reason to love Mussoorie - it was home to his favorite author, Ruskin Bond. From a young age, Avi had been captivated by Bond's writing on the beauty of nature and the hills. He loved the way Bond ended his stories and the suspense and thrill he woven into them.

Avi had read many of Bond's books and short stories, but his all-time favorite was "The Eyes Have It."

Chakrata, on the other hand, is also a hill station, around 90 kms from Mussorie with approx. three hours' drive. Avi was quite busy these days, so he was least interested in any trip. Avi declined the offer citing his low leave balances and work pressure. But Ajeet was in no mood to hear a "No", apparently. "Avi, you know, you can take advance privilege leaves as well. The HR people will deduct these leaves from you PL of next year. How cool it is. Listen brother, the trip is commencing next week from Sunday. So practically, you need to take just two days off! Plus, you can finish your work by sitting late this week, you have sufficient days to tackle that. Trust me buddy, this trip will be one helluva trip of our lifetimes. We will meet new people, girls!!! Who knows after few years where we end up? Some of us would get married with boring life and big paunch sitting on these office chairs like sticked with glue. Amid those long and gloomy faces, these memories will come as saviours. And that time you will remember me, that you had one friend, Ajeet, who took you out of this pile of shit to live some moments for your own. Come on, you can just not say "No". No, No's are allowed, final". Avi said Yes to the trip at the end, less for the excitement Ajeet showed, but more to shut his big fat mouth.

The week went fine for Avi. As Ajeet had suggested, he worked for some extra hours where he could get the work done smoothly. And since the work was in balance, the bosses allowed him 2 days leave without any hesitation. Avi, finally, was now happy for this upcoming trip. Little did he knew what kind of experience is waiting for him in the hillocks of Mussoorie and Chakrata.

Chapter 3

Taravi

> Secretly, he was looking for her,
> So, the cosmos showered the planner,
> A bestowal, was to fall into his kitty,
> She is, his, serendipity!!!

The trip was about to commence for Mussoorie and Chakrata the next day. Ajeet was briefing the whole travel plan to Avi. "Bud, the itinerary is like, we will depart at morning 9:00 AM from Doon and around 10:30 AM we will reach Mussoorie. The bus will wait for us at Clock Tower. We will go straight to the Kempty falls where we would spend around two to three hours. Then will come to Mall Road and spend the rest of the day. After spending the night in a resort, we would go to Dhanaulti the next day in morning, post breakfast. Then, we will go to Company Garden. From there we will proceed to Chakrata where we shall have a party and rest for the night. The next and the last day, was dedicated to Chakrata. The places like tiger fall and some of the caves we shall cover. And after that, back to Dehradun!"

"Aren't we going to see "Winter line" of Mussorie?", Avi asked. Mussoorie is famous for its winter line which is seen from Mall Road. It is a formation of line at the time of sunset on the horizon, which is a mix of golden, orange, and blue colours taking it from the Sun and the sky. This phenomenon is visible at around sunset in winters only. Ajeet confirmed that when they will cover Mall Road, they shall be covering it as well.

On 16th, everyone assembled at clock tower including Ajeet and Avi. It was a small tour of around 40 people from people around the lengths and breadths of the country. Some were on time, while others were a little late. They were among the early comers. Ajeet wanted to sit in the front as playboy in him was roaring high. While he, chose the back seats. Avi enjoyed some solitude in the laps of nature to enjoy it away from the commotion. Avi took him, forcefully, to the back seats, against of course Ajeet's wishes. The bus started to fill up. The rolls were called, and everyone had made it to the bus. Avi was lost in the statue of clock tower and the traffic around. How the statute was silently standing in the centre doing his job without any effort. People are passing by around it, but it is unmoved, unaffected, silent, calm, doing its work without any effort or show off. Wish we could be like it.

He didn't like traffic throughout his life but, somehow, he could never feel the same for Dehradun's. In this hustle and bustle, he still could feel the vibes of love. The city always exuded oodles of love. Even when the place is choc a bloc with vehicles, Avi was finding it beautiful. Crazy!

Avi's dream was broken when he felt a side blow on his chest. It was Ajeet. His mouth was open with saliva dropping down from his upper side of the mouth to the lower, eyes wide open and a bizarre smile on his face as if he was longing for a chicken and he got chicken tikka with chicken pop corns and a diet soda. He gave a blow to Avi again and asked him to see at his nearby seat, after the passage in the middle of the bus. There was a girl, well yeah beautiful, who was sitting on that seat which made Ajeet go gaga. Avi gave him a long and stern look like, what are you upto dude. Ajeet expressions like, well yeah, as if we are supposed to be here for something else. Ajeet being Ajeet, Avi being Avi.

The trip embarked to Mussoorie. Avi was on the window seat and while Ajeet was busy in checking on each girl of the bus, he was busy watching the nature on the hill ride from Dehradun to Mussoorie. The mountains had another impact on him always. The vegetation of mountains and the views always made him awestruck. The air striking on the face as if kissing and gone in fraction of time. People passing by, waving hands, saying hello or bidding farewell, who knows. The trees looked like as if they are going back saying a lovely goodbye, or a reminder that nothing stays forever. The past is gone, and the future is uncertain. All you have is the present moment. Carpe Diem, Seize the moment!!!

They reached Kempty Falls on time. Since the traffic was not much that day, they managed to get to the place on time even when they started half an hour late. It is a water fall in the lap of nature, where one need to head down on some steps on a hilly track to reach there. The place is not just beautiful, but the icy cold waters make you go numb and gives a kick. Avi had brought his swim wears along. He got it changed in a changing room nearby and went into the waterfalls. Whoa!!! The water was very cold. He took a fast dip so that his body gets accustomed to the chill that waters brought with them. Soon his body adapted to the temperature of water. Ajeet was on the other side, busy finding his future sweetheart. Avi was enjoying his own company. He was having his time in the falls when suddenly a harsh gush of water fell onto his chest from the top of the falls. In haste he moved to one side where he bumped into someone. He apologised to the person immediately while still drenched in the water.

"That water was really harsh, isn't it" a voice cranked.

It was the most melodious voice he ever heard. He wiped those waters from his eyes and saw her. He went awestruck. What did just happen!! Was he in a dream, as he never saw someone so beautiful in his entire life. He said sorry again. "I had heard you the first time. No need to say that you did not do it intentionally" said the girl with a smile on her face. She turned back to go other way and Avi in all confusion could not understand what to say and amidst all this confusion with a slur in his mouth and a racing heart, he asked, "Hey, I could not catch your name".

"Well, you could not catch it, as I never mentioned it" she said it with a chuckle. Putting her sunglasses on, she said while turning, "Tara, Tara Sharma". And she was going. Avi could not move a muscle. He was just looking at her dumbstruck. He could not ask anything else. He could not fathom what to speak. He had butterflies in the belly and an intangible anchor at his feet. He was like a mad man seeing her drifting away, slowly, and slowly. He was back to his senses when he felt a mild blow on his back. "Where are you lost my friend. Let's have something to eat. I am hungry!" Ajeet exclaimed. They had some omelettes and tea to quench the hunger while Avi was still in hangover with mesmerising beauty of Tara.

They changed their clothes and went up to the bus. Avi went on to have a fag of smoke. While he was smoking at the joint, he saw Tara, again. Tara was entering the bus. Wait, isn't this bus the same bus in which they travelled from Dehradun till here. "What?? She was in the same bus with me all this time. And where was I. I did not even know." Avi was shocked.

He finished his smoke halfway, had some mouth freshener and went inside the bus. Tara was sitting on the second row of seats. "Shoot!! Why on earth I chose to sit on the last seats, today!!!" Avi was making his way to his seat exchanging glances with Tara.

"Hey, even I didn't catch your name" Avi moved around. It was Tara who was asking him this with a smile on her face.

"Avi. It is Avi here." he said excitedly.

"It's nice meeting you Avi. I hope you are okay."

"Yeah, absolutely. It was a harsh blow, but thankfully, I was saved. I am completely fine. Thanks for asking." Avi smiled.

"So, all by yourself in the trip?" Tara Asked.

"No, have come with one of my friends, Ajeet. How about you?"

"I like going on solo trips or people with whom the frequency matches. Friends whom I connect with, were kind of busy. But maybe this is how it has to be. Nothing happens randomly. I believe in the cosmic plan." Tara said all this with a serene and mystical smile on her face leaving Avi spellbound to not just her words, but the charm she brought with that.

Ajeet broke in. "Hey, I am Ajeet, Avi's friend. He must have told you about me." with a wink. Tara exchanged pleasantries with Ajeet while Avi was looking at her like a child looks at stars, in the night, thinking one day he will be able to touch them, feel them, when he will grow big. "Ajeet, why don't you take the seats. I will just come." Avi said. With a perplexed look, Ajeet went to his seat.

"Your friend is interesting" Tara teased.

"Well, he is on a different voyage" Avi winked.

People started coming back and taking their seats. A guy came and saw Tara, smiled, and he tried his way to seat next to her. Tara introduced him to Avi, "This is Rahul, my seatmate in this trip." Rahul and Avi shook hands and greeted. Avi so wanted to sit next to her, but! He moved to his seat giving a smile to Tara. The bus torqued again towards Mall Road.

The whole time till they reached Mall Road, Avi was lost in the image of Tara. Her hairs flowing in air, when she wore those sunglasses, the water coming down from her forehead making its way through her eyes, her nose, her cheeks, her lips, and her chin. How beautiful she is, as if, she was made in the upper worlds when the almighty was in the best of his moods. So, he chose the best of whatever is required, to make her and filled her with so much innocence, beauty, charm, and love. Avi was feeling high on admiration of her. When and how they reached Mall Road, he had no idea. As he started to disembark bus, he saw sulking face of Ajeet. Avi took him to the betel shop nearby to share a smoke to lighten up his mood. They started exploring Mall Road when Avi saw Tara standing under a gazebo on sides of the mall road. Avi asked Ajeet to continue and strolled his way towards Tara. She was facing towards the valley, her eyes closed, a beautiful smile on her face, her hands open wide, having slow but long enough breather, as if her whole body became one with the nature. Her stole waving with the flow of the wind in her hands. She was looking like a divine beauty, exuding divine lights from her Aura and he got lost in her. So much, that he did not even know when Tara came close to him and shook him. She had a surprising smile on her face and was like, "What? What happened? Why you were looking at me in stupor!". Avi could not say a word, he just smiled and asked her to let's go ahead. Probably, Tara understood.

"You like nature? You, kind of, were lost in it there." Avi asked.

"Well, who doesn't? Don't you like nature? Don't these mountains look like to you as if some yogi is sitting in *sadhana,* unmoved, unaffected since eons. The wind that is blowing as if touching you, rejuvenating each cell of your body. As if it wants you to take the flight, leaving all your worries aside. Forget about what is happening around, and just fly, high, high as you can. Touch those clouds, go merry go round around the sun. Paint the whole canvas, the Sky, in the colour you want. You are on your own, for yourself, with yourself. Isn't it beautiful Avi?" Tara said it all with a twinkle in her eyes. Avi could not agree more. But the way Tara described it in that moment he knew one thing, he won't be able to stop himself from falling in love with her.

"So, Tell me about you. I have been doing all the talking all this while. You are being so secretive. Come on, spill the beans!" Tara asked.

"What? I am an open book. And book can't talk." Avi said with a lame laughter.

"A book speaks the best! I hope this book opens soon to me." Tara walked ahead saying this, wearing a mysterious smile on her face, again, and upping her sunglasses to her eyes.

"Why don't you read it on your own then?", Avi asked from behind, while trailing her.

"Who said I am not reading?", Tara responded leaving Avi perplexed.

"Okay, well, and what does your reading say then?" Avi asked this with a rested smile and deepness in his eyes.

"Well, you are a person who reserves most of the things to himself. No body, and I repeat, no body, knows you, at least, under the sun. You hide a lot and sometimes wear a mask on your face so that people don't know your vulnerabilities. You are afraid to get hurt. You are someone who wants to fly high and free, but still not being able to leave the ground. Someone with wings but trapped in a cage. Someone, who so wants to break free through these shackles of the society. Reason, at times family, other times, the society or any tom, dick and harry who he gives power to. But not able to do because of fear and lack of bit self-love. You often ponder, is this world not right or am I the one who is a misfit here? Do I belong to an old school where people feel from heart?", Tara said it all in one breath. Avi was dumbfounded.

"Well, that's one for the book, but you hardly know me, this much even my own family and friends don't know", Avi was bit shocked.

'Well, I guess I have this gift to read people', Tara fluttered.

Whatever Tara said, it like triggered lot of buried questions inside him. He was suddenly lost in it when Tara asked, "What are you thinking Avi, share with me".

"Why on earth everyone is living so materialistically here. Why they can spend bomb in temples or giving alms in some charity function or at some other place, but don't let those people touch them even. Is it a compassion or a transaction to settle the karmas, as if, not doing some charity will not reserve them seats inside those pearly gates of heaven? Why they want to accumulate so much when they know they won't be able to take anything along. Why there are so much of judgements and opinions everywhere, even from those whom I call my family, my closest friends. Why we just can't accept people, situations as they are. Why they always are looking for a version which suits their narratives?", Avi said it all with poise.

"Before addressing these questions outside to the society and people around you, why not let us do some internal analysis for own selves? For instance, have you ever wondered, why do you smoke? Not to look cool, but thinking it might help to dwindle away from these hard-hitting deep blocks you are carrying inside you. Instead of facing it, you are like running away from it by engaging in all these addictions. You love drinking so that your mind can find some peace in all this chaos, outside as well as inside, so that you can fall asleep in that inebriated state, avoiding all the commotion".

"I think you are right Tara, these dependency on addictions are because we are simply running away, afraid to face our inner demons," Avi admitted.

"There is more to it. I also feel inside you have some passion or interest long hidden but couldn't follow it, like you wanted to be a doctor but doing law, why?"

"I don't know, but yeah, you are right, I wanted to be a singer, song writer, also a traveller, but my family never supported me because of their conditionings and expectation from me" he said with a tinch of sadness.

"But did you even try to take stand of what you want to be? Since it is your life, choice must be yours. What gives you contentment and joy?" she asked calmly.

"Frankly, I did not take that much stand, I was too busy pleasing them because of my own apprehensions. I know I was never able to say a word to them in a discussion or argument and accepted everything they say, even when they were wrong." He sighed with a sudden realisation how unfair he has been to himself.

Tara further continued, "You also want to cry, at times loud, but don't, fearing people will read your emotions and how will you respond to the questions they would pose. So, you block everyone out. You are so much trapped in these realms that you have made a wall inside you, may be because of some traumas and pains of childhood. You have shut your heart and now it looks like a maze to reach to your heart. Open gate one, then second and so on and then only one can find real Avi, who is sitting on a bank of some lake or river, playing a flute with a beautiful smile, completely by himself, feeling love for himself, without any notions or thoughts about the society or the people around him. Can I be with that Avi in these two days, the real Avi?" Tara's tone going from strong, to soft, as she finished speaking.

Avi went short of breath. As if, someone had hit him hard where it really hurts. Someone gave him a mirror to let him see the real him. Someone who has been hiding for so long. Avi knew, Tara was right, but he did not expect her to read him so well. He was awestruck and at the same time like in a face palm situation. As if someone slapped him so hard but with all the softness and tenderness. To deviate from the topic, Avi started making some funny face and said, "What should I do now?".

"Take a dip in Lake Chaubunagungamaug", Tara muttered.

"Wait, what is that?", Avi asked.

"You have got google in your phone!!!", Tara said roughly while walking.

"Touché!!", Avi said fervently.

They discussed a lot more things while walking on the road ranging from aspirations, childhood dreams, favourite author, favourite movie, favourite actor & actresses, hobbies, music genre, bands, dream destinations and what not. They got along well. They had so much common shared interests and it seemed like they could spend days talking and talking without even a drop of fatigue. They saw the beautiful winter line together, took a lot of photographs, shared laughs. The two were enjoying the company of each other. Initially it was Avi who was stealing glances of Tara, now it was Tara as well, who was getting drawn to his charm, sense of humour, simplicity, intensity & honesty he had in him. His eyes were deep, like one could travel all the way to his soul through them. But somehow, still closed to the larger audience. Will it open for Tara? Only time can tell.

On the way back to hotel Tara was lost in her own thoughts. She had a knack this connect is not just normal two days fling but much deeper. She had met many people in her life who were like minded, nature lovers, adventurous but there was something about him that she was getting attracted to him. Many times, she felt déjà vu like she knows him somehow and have met him before. She was aware that he has blocked his heart because of various factors, but when he will open and the love that will flow, it will surpass all limitations. When he looked at her or smiled at her, not only she felt shudders and goosebumps but also something in her heart. She wanted to follow her inner voice even when mind was revolting to go ahead. But even in all that, she felt home in him.

The day was about to end, and it was time to go to the resort. They checked in to their rooms and had dinner. As everyone was tired so soon people started going to their rooms for sleep. Tara too was sleepy, though Avi wanted to chat with her more, but could see the fatigue in her eyes. So, he ushered her to her room. They stood there for some time, smiling at each other, as if, the eyes were talking to each other. It was getting mildly cold. Finally, Tara took her hand out to shake and said "Good Night, Avi. It was a beautiful day spent with you."

"The pleasure was mine, Madame." "Ciao!! Good night, sleep well, and Avi Dreams." Avi said with a wink and a smile. Tara could not help but had the broadest smile on her face and with that they parted for the day.

While Avi was lost in the memories with a smile on bed as insomniac of him was not able to sleep, on the other hand, Tara too, was, contagiously, not being able to sleep. She too was lost in this hassle of heart and mind. Don't know when and how, they managed to sleep in the silence of nature.

***

After having a sumptuous breakfast at resort, the caravan moved to Dhanaulti. It is a small hill range near Mussorie. People who go to Mussoorie, do go to Dhanaulti to see the nature, tall oak, and deodar trees and of course, snow. It still had some snow, left over from the last night fall. Avi and Tara were having gala time together, played with snow, making snowballs, and throwing it on each other. Lost in their own world, they were having the time of their lives!

"Avi. What does this snow feel to you like?"

"Ummm!! A water that has frozen, that we enjoy throwing on each other, icy cold, feels so good on hand. I wonder how it would feel if I take it inside my T-Shirt, wooohoo.."

"Hmmm!!!"

"Sorry, you wanted me to answer differently?"

"Take a piece of snow in your hands. Now, close your eyes. Feel the softness it has. Feel how it is melting in your hands, like a sufi music penetrating deep inside your ears and going straight to your soul, through your heart. Let the melting water find its way on its own and take your consciousness there. Feel that water is getting one with your body, like your body is absorbing it wherever it is flowing. Now, feel its energy flowing inside your body through your hands, your palms, to veins, everywhere. Feel it flowing inside, touching, and rejuvenating every cell of your body. And when you are done, slowly open your eyes".

"What was that?" asked trancey Avi, something he never felt before or even thought to feel nature in this way. He was perplexed how a small thing like this can kindle those sensations inside which he did not even know he had. He was feeling so giddy, as if, he had two pegs of scotch on an empty stomach. His head was heavy and calm at the same time. He had immense pressure on middle of his forehead.

"Where had you been all this while?" he teased her.

"In your dreams" she teased back.

It was time, to move to the next destination, company garden. It is also known as municipal garden. The garden has variety of flowers, scenic views, and some fountains. Avi was still in a trance; he had got from that snow thing Tara asked him to do. Tara knew what Avi was going through.

"Don't worry, this will go. You felt like this for the first time, isn't it? Happens. Don't worry. I hope you liked it though", Tara said.

"It was beautiful. I can still feel some sensations inside. As if there is an adrenaline rush quivering inside whole of my body, a gush of fresh energy flowing within. This is better than those daily vitamins I am taking to be honest. But this pain on middle of my forehead, uff!!!"

"Wait, let me see. Sit here, on this bench." Tara said.

They sat on a bench in the garden. Tara asked Avi to sit cross legged on the bench and she sat in front of him, eyes closed. How beautiful she is, Avi was talking to self, inside in his mind seeing her sitting eyes closed in front of him. Tara, suddenly, raised her hand and took it to his forehead, on the middle. Her hands started waving in clockwise position.

"Close your eyes and take your consciousness on your forehead, especially, between the eyebrows." Tara said it in a very soft and subtle tone. Avi did the same, as was told.

"Now open your eyes", after 20 seconds or so Tara asked Avi. "How does it feel there? Is there any pain still left?" Tara asked.

"Holy Moly!! There is no pain. All gone!!! What did you do???"

Tara chuckled "Nothing just calmed your head a little with loving energies."

Avi's mouth was so wide open, one could count not just all the teeth but also could test the cavities, without having any degree in dentistry.

"Ahh, Okay. Hehe. Can understand your expressions well. Let me try to explain it to you. Umm, see this drainpipe near you, from which the excess water of this fountain is flowing. Can you see the water flowing in this conduit?"

"Yes, I can" he said cluelessly.

"What would happen if I put a big stone in between the water flow inside this conduit?"

"The water will stop flowing and also the dirt and moss will start accumulating near that stone".

"Exactly, my boy!! In the same way, because you experienced pure nature energy, it kind of pushed the impure energy of emotional and mental conduits which gave you this pressure." She said with a radiant smile.

Avi had no clue what she was saying, nor he wanted to have because he was so lost staring her, the way her eyes twinkled, the way she rolled her lips.. her lips… he so wanted to touch them, her pink cheeks he wanted to caress, he started to feel as he was high on alcohol without drinking a single drop.

"Avi!" Tara jolted him "where are you lost?"

"In you" he said without thinking.

"What?" she couldn't contain her smile and the blush that followed.

"You are feeling better now, right?" Tara asked.

"Indeed. Never felt this better in my life before to be honest. I have had migraine issues and have been using a lot of pain killers for headache. It's like once a week I pop some pill to cure this pain inside my head. But trust me, this was better than any pain killers. Can you make a contract that whenever I will feel this pain you will do this woosh woosh on my forehead. Can you please?" He folded his hands and sat down on his knees.

Tara crackled while she held his hands and made him stand up, "Can't promise!"

Tara and Avi clicked a lot of pictures there. After spending some time there and lunch, they moved to their next destination, Chakrata. Chakrata is a cantonment area and lies on west of Mussorie, a hilly range. The road has a beautiful view of mountains to its sides along with long oak trees. It is approximately a 90-100 kms drive from Mussorie.

When they reached Chakrata, the night had already dawned. A bon fire party was arranged at the resort for the group. After getting freshen up, everyone met at the gardens for bon fire and music.

There was a live band performing. The band was playing some soft sensuous romantic numbers, both Hindi and English. Everyone was enjoying, and Tara Avi were smiling to each other while listening to the songs and were flowing.

"Love this vibe", Tara said with a soft and warm smile on her face, looking at Avi, as if her eyes made a union with his eyes in that very moment. Their eyes, as if glued to each other, the whole world went blurry in the backdrop, it was just him and her, and that moment. The words had no role whatsoever, as the eyes were enough to do all the talking. Two oceans were merging, through their eyes.

"It's beautiful", Avi responded after a while, slightly coming out of that tipsy like state of flowing emotions, amidst revellers around.

"Why don't you sing a song, your hidden passion" she said.

"I am not that a great singer, Tara".

"Don't lie to me. Your eyes speak volumes that you love it when you sing".

"Hehe. Yeah, you are right. I don't know how to play any instrument though but yeah; I do like singing. But I am not a very competent singer. I have not got any training in that, a mediocre one, but I love to sing for my own self. It's like, it gives me roots and drenches my soil or soul. It is my way of balancing my inner core you can say" Avi winked.

"So, come on sing a song" She insisted.

"No way. Am not going to that stage".

"Who asked you to go there?"

"Then?" he asked surprisingly.

"Sing a song here, for me" she said with childlike sparkle in her eyes.

That look in her eyes, that smile, that grace, that charm, that beauty, that yearning, that devotion, that submission, that belongingness, that flow, that said unsaid, made him sing without any reluctance.

[2]"नैना तेरे कजरारे है, नैनो पे हम दिल हारे है,

अनजाने ही तेरे नैनो ने, वादे किये कई सारे है,

साँसों की लय, मद्धम चलें

तोसे कहे,

बरसेगा सावन, बरसेगा सावन

झूम झूमके,

दो दिल ऐसे मिलेंगे

आओगे जब तुम ओ साजना

अंगना फूल खिलेंगे|"

The moment froze. Both, of them, could not speak a word. Completely lost in each other. It was just them. Everything else, just did not seem to exist, at all. Tara could not help but left that gaze and turned her face to other side to grasp her breath again. Avi too turned his face down and started making some imaginary drawings on the table with his fingers. It was peculiar of him. Whenever he gets a flood of emotions, his fingers start playing on anything stable, automatically. After a while, Tara turned her gaze towards him, again. Her eyes were wet but had an alluring smile and loads of love flowing towards Avi.

"Know what, a lot of people have given me letters, have wrote poetries, done the weirdest things ever possible for a human and all that stuff, but this, what you did just now. It is the most beautiful thing happened to me in my life. Not because you sing well, which by the way you do. But for the feel it had. Those emotions touched my soul. You have

---

[2] song from Jab we met

touched my soul. Maximum people could reach till my spirit only. You are the only one who could touch my soul, Avi. Thank you! I don't have words. What I am feeling right now, no number of words can exactly describe it, for words carry a limited meaning." Tara held his hands after saying it all, and they sat there for some moments.

"Excuse me for a minute", Avi asked her, and she nodded. She understood, maybe he needs time to process those emotions. In the meantime, she started checking her phone, trying to come back to this real world, while Avi went for a break. She was herself like flying high, as if suddenly her heart had wings. Her heart, mind, each cell of body like was still bathing in this strange feeling called, may be love. She asked herself, is this love? Since her school time she had a vague experience of it, like that rush for her crush, going weak in knees with her first kiss, feeling those butterflies when someone proposed her. But this was different, this was like someone came and just touched deepest part of her soul with so much simplicity that made her heart flow like anything. Like stream of river was literally flowing in her heart when he looked in her eyes and held her hands. This feel, even some intimate moments couldn't make her feel in past. A ping from her parents broke her transcendental flow. She was like welcome to the real world again, with all the chuckles. She heard some abrupt noise of mic setting on the stage, which she ignored while replying to some of the texts and texting her parents that she is fine and has reached Chakrata well.

"Good evening, guys!!" A voice echoed from stage which sounded familiar. Is it, OMG, Avi?

"I hope you are having a great evening." Avi said to which the crowd cheered in unison.

"I want to sing a song, not for a person, but for the most beautiful soul, I ever met in my entire life" and Avi sang a song, 'She', a number from Elvis Costello.

Tara could not hold her tears back. She could not believe Avi would go on stage for her, singing a song! Her eyes got closed a several times in between, flowing with his voice. She was so lost, as if she was travelling in some other world altogether. It was like a realm in some other dimension where she felt she knew and have been there. It was a huge grassland like field with beautiful white flowers all around. She saw a huge tree in between the grassland, the tree was shining, beaming. From the tree one swing is hanging down from one of the branches and she saw two people sitting on it. She tried to look more closely, gosh! Its them, she, and Avi. Swinging slowly and totally lost in each other, Tara has kept her head on the shoulder of Avi. The moon is illuminating so bright from the horizon and stars engulfing the whole sky. First, she saw Avi wearing a black tux and she, a red gown. But then as she was going deeper and deep by becoming one with the music, she suddenly saw them in different form. He, wearing a white silver dress like a Greek god while she is wearing the brightest white silver gown she has ever seen. She almost looked like a Greek goddess as well. She didn't want her mind to speculate. What is she seeing? It was certainly not her imagination, because conscious mind can only imagine what it has seen in their life. While this on the other hand she never even thought she will ever imagine.

They were just lost in love, not human love, but some divine or cosmic love, a cosmic leela which knew no form or boundaries. It just knows, Love! And it was flowing, purely and piously, between them, there, in that world. Like nothing else mattered in that moment. It was so vivid. As she opened her eyes, they were wet, Avi was still singing, looking at her with all that love. Tara smiled, lovingly, seeing him, not just for his singing, but what she experienced just now. She felt she had the most amazing glimpse of her entire life, may be her home in some higher realm, perhaps their higher selves?? Avi finished singing, everyone clapped, including Tara. He came back to the table, smiling with love. Tara was smiling too, but Avi could get it that there is something unusual in that smile, something else.

"What happened?", Avi asked.

"Can we go to some quiet place, away from here, this fuss. I know one place, let's go there.", Tara took Avi holding his hands. The resort was on a hill and the rooms were also placed like that. Some rooms were on this upside and some down. She took him to a place, from where the whole valley was visible. There was a single bench there under a tree, with a number engraved, 594. Tara smiled seeing a bench under a tree reminding her of what she saw just now.

"I saw something while you were singing on the podium, and I want you to listen to that please." Tara said.

"What do you mean you saw something? You mean something happened there while I was singing?" Avi asked.

Tara smiled. "Yes, something happened, not there, but inside of me. I had my first partial out of body experience."

"You had What???", Avi stood up hollering.

"Relax! Let me explain it to you. At times of deep trance, or meditative state, we do have visions and also our spirit can travel out of body to some other realms. It is possible. And it is not an imagination, you can read autobiographies and biographies of famous yogis like Paramhansa Yogananda, Lahri Mahsya Jee, Mahavtar Babaji to count a few. And guess what, I met with our higher selves", Tara said it all with so much excitement. Avi on the other side, was in a shudder.

"Higher selves?"

"Yeah, higher self. Or maybe divine selves or cosmic selves, I don't know. Need to ponder on that." Tara said.

"Now what is divine and cosmic self. Mind explaining please, if you can't see I am still gasping for breath", Avi said.

"Hehe. Okay. Let me explain. Our soul was created up above, by the creators or say *Paramatma*. That pure raw form that is spark of the creator is also called cosmic or divine selves which is almost like God. Then it descends to have various experiences and help other souls. So divine self descends to higher selves. These forms can be lighter higher self and dark higher self. For example, we have 'Shiva - The Adiyogi' but also a form of his as destructive too 'Mahakal' which is also important for cleansing to give way to new seeds. Same goes with shakti, a compassionate mother, yet fierce kali to slay demons. These demons are also inside us, the dark virtues like greed, anger etc. I feel the spirit realms above the seven lokas as we read in Hindu scriptures is where our higher selves exist. Like the demigods, angels, masters, spirit guides etc. Then part of our higher self chooses to take human birth, to learn more lessons, transform our dark virtues to light ones and evolve. In this journey as humans, we take "N" number of births to have different experiences and each birth should be one step to climb up, to go back to our abode. As we grow, become aware, we start merging with our higher self and I feel this power of love what I felt took me very deep and I had a vision of higher selves. Perhaps right now they are existing in that beautiful realm, lost in love, as we meet here and are experiencing it. You know like we see in movies, a parallel universe, a version of us existing somewhere else too. Just this is not a human birth version but higher self. Oh! By the way we looked cool in those attires like some godly prince and princess.", Tara said it all with a broad smile and twinkle in her eyes.

"Okay, getting it a little. What did they say to you?", Avi understood a bit but more he was lost in that childlike twinkle she was exuding from her eyes and that made him filled with so much joy and more love for her.

"Well, they did not say anything, but I saw them doing something", Tara said with a wink. Then she explained him everything she saw and experienced, that ocean, that tree, that swing, them sitting on that swing, her face on his shoulder, Moonlit sky, Stars, their godly appearances, everything. Avi was astonished and was lost in all what he heard. Suddenly, Tara held his hands and kept them in her laps, while seeing the view ahead of them of the valley. She slowly ushered "Baby, you are magician, your love made me experience what I couldn't ever. I feel so blessed and your love is magical".

Avi looked at her, she looked at him, as usual, the eyes were doing all the talking. There was stillness in the atmosphere, except the sound of the breeze, birds, like whole nature was dancing with them in these silent whispers of love. Avi could not stop himself, leaned ahead, and kissed her forehead and her eyes. Tara's eyes closed for a moment. The love was flowing eternally. Avi rested his head on her shoulder and Tara started caressing his hairs while tilting her head on his. Avi took her hands in his, and started playing with them, making shape of heart and writing letters A and T on her palms, pressing his palms gently on hers. Her hands were so soft and supple. That touch was touching his heart, straight away. Tara was feeling no different. Mingling her fingers with his, like they were making a bond, a bond for a lifetime, and beyond. Avi took her hand close to his heart, and a flood of emotions broke. He kissed her hands and was rubbing them with his. His eyes were a little moist. He leaned more and lied on her laps, seeing her face from there. Tara made him lie comfortably and started caressing his head and brushing his hairs with her hands. They were seeing each other like the time had stopped and this moment is forever. Tara bent forward and kissed him on his forehead. Avi's eyes closed for a moment. This kissed melted him from inside. His heart, as if, had become soft like a melting wax. As if waves are flowing on his whole heart. He started brushing her hairs, lying from her laps, and massaging her scalp with his fingers. They stayed like this for a while.

"It is late now. We have to get up early for tomorrow. Let's go for sleep now.", Tara kept brushing his hairs with her hands while saying all this.

"Let's wait for some time, please. Let's bask in this warmth for some time", Avi pleaded like a kid.

"No! Get up", Tara made him get up. Her dress had gone all ruffled up on the laps, as he was lying there. She pressed it up a little with her hands and after a decent attempt to make it like before, she looked up at Avi. He had an anguished face, like a baby is angry for not getting a chocolate.

"Awww,", and she kissed him on his cheeks. "Now, okay?", Tara said, wearing a sweet smile.

"Never this better", Avi said with an even broader smile. They both chuckled.

They walked back to their rooms, which were nearby, holding each other's hands in their arms.

"Good night", Tara said from the gate of her room, which was half shut, half open. "This was the best day of my life", Tara continued.

"Good night. This was the best day of my entire soul journey.", Avi responded with a wink. "Avi Dreams"

They both chuckled as they parted their way.

Though they went to their respective rooms to find some sleep but were not able to, at all. The whole day was like running in flash in front of them. A lot of beautiful moments were running in front, as if a movie is running on the silver screen.

Tara was still tossing and turning on her bed. Two hours had passed by, already, and she could not sleep, smiling all the way. Suddenly her phone had a ping. It was a text from Avi, a rather long text.

I could hear the birds chirping,

the music of air passing through leaves,

You were there, sitting besides me,

As if we met after a life's time.

Looking into your eyes, those eyes,

which were yearning for me since long,

That touch of your hand, it felt so strong.

My resting the head on your shoulders,

Pressing your hands, playing with your fingers,

Keeping them close to my heart,

as if GOD answered all my prayers.

That Kissing your forehead, kissing your hand,
It was as if somebody played a wand,
In that very moment of stillness,
It was just you and me,
I could hear you all,
and you could hear me.

There were people passing by,
And we were so engrossed in hearing each other's sigh,
The moment we can cherish forever,
That bench No. 594 will always be on my mind.

The day, we waited, a cosmos boon,
I wanted it to stay forever, but it ended so soon.
A day which was a paradigm of oxymoron,
Where something gone missing and some where we became one.

I could not leave to say goodbye,
That love and sadness were closest ally,
You were mine and I was yours to the core,
somehow someway, am still on that bench no 594.

It was last day of the trip but seems as if the journey had just started for Tara and Avi. They met each other at the dining area for breakfast with sleepy eyes, smiling at each other. The love was still flowing effervescently between them. Tara was ahead of him in the queue for food and just like that she turned back looking deeply in his eyes and said, "That poem, it just took my breath away". Avi kept looking at her with a smile. They took their breakfast together.

The group started for Tiger Falls at 9. Avi requested Rahul to exchange seats with him, of course, against the wishes of Ajeet. Tara too wanted the same but did not say. Rahul was gracious enough to exchange the seats. Tara held Avi's hands in her, and they both stared out of the window to have those breath-taking views of the journey to the falls.

Tiger Falls is one of the pristine falls. The trek is difficult, though has stairs, but is quite a long trek. But the views are amazing not just at the falls but during the whole journey.

After walking for 10 minutes, Avi was like, "What a long arduous trek it is. Especially with these sleepy eyes" chuckled Avi.

"Is it still arduous when am with you?", Tara teased him.

"No No, I mean, it's nice and beautiful to be with you in this trek. But still, it is tiring to the legs. And we are walking downhill. Don't know what will happen when we shall return as it shall be an uphill walk then. Feeling those tremors in my legs already", Avi babbled.

"You know what the most beautiful thing about a journey is?", Tara asked it with a smile.

"Well, the destination where we are heading towards. Like here, the falls. The views shall be so mesmerising I know for sure. All tiredness shall be gone once we shall reach there and see those serene falls", Avi gushed.

"No"

"Then?"

"It's the journey that matters, not the stops or the milestones or the destination".

"We keep searching for happiness in events, like when this will happen, I will be happy. We have this preconceived notion that some event or an achievement will make me happy, and, in the process, we stop feeling the beauty of the journey all along. See the views Avi, see these plants, this greenery, the air- so fresh and embracing, these colours all-around of flowers, grass, huts, clothes of people here, sky, horizon; the sun giving us that bright light over the mountains, our being together. Enjoy the journey, Avi, and destination will never be a task to achieve, isn't it? Who cares what lies at the end? A beautiful waterfall or a small pond. All that matters is what we have right now. What we are experiencing right now. The present moment is all we have. Let us not waste our time in thinking about what shall happen next, rather, let us be in the flow. Or rather, be the flow?" Tara Exclaimed.

Avi kept looking at Tara in amusement. It was like as if she is refreshing the learnings he has long forgotten. He then took a whole view of the valley. Indeed, how beautiful it was. Avi opened his arms to become one with the nature. To merge himself in it. He was listening to those sounds; he had no idea existed. The coo of the birds was never this clear. The water from a stream nearby, the air passing through, someone singing a song from a nearby village, some whistling sound from a pressure cooker in nearby hut, and what's that? What this sound is? Lub dub lub dub. Avi tried to feel it closely with his eyes closed. The voice was coming from inside of him. "Whoa! That's my heartbeat." Avi had a tear drop in his eyes with a beautiful smile, strangely.

Avi was feeling so much love not just for Tara but for like everything and everyone crossing his paths. He was saying hello to people, having this "Awwww" feeling for everyone. A constant smile was there on his lips.

They reached the falls after some time. The sound of waters falling was amazing. Tara could feel the purity of love flow Avi had just discovered inside. She was happy, may be more than Avi. Suddenly a splash of water touched her face, and she was out of dream in no time. It was Avi. He was playful like a kid. Tara retorted with throwing water on Avi. Avi sided and missed. "Na-na Na-na Na-na", Avi Teased.

Tara started running for him like wait and I will punch you on your face. Avi was running ahead laughing incessantly and Tara running after him, showing him her fist in playful manner. Avi stopped at the end of falls where there was a large pond as there was no place left to go further. Tara could not stop in sync, and she bumped into him. They both fell into the waters. Everyone started laughing at them seeing them in the pool of waters. The water was falling from up above in the pool. Both had a shy laugh for what just happened. Avi then threw some more water on her from the pool. Tara was like, "You still don't want to stop. Wait!!" They both played a lot with water. Suddenly Tara's feet got slipped on a mossy stone beneath she was unaware due to unclear waters. She was about to tumble when Avi held her immediately. Tara was safe. She saw Avi while still swinging on his arms and Avi too kept staring at her. It was looking like that typical Bollywood movie somewhat like RK Films logo where Raj Kapoor held Nargis in his arms except that Tara was looking at Avi and not away.

Avi made Tara come up and stand on her feet, but he could not move his arms from her body. He was still holding her from her waist. The time had stopped, yet again. Everything had frozen. It was just them and the sound of waters falling into the pool. They were looking at each other and the drops of water were trickling down from their faces. Avi moved his right hand to her face to wipe those waters from her face and detangled and brushed her hairs with his hand. It was all love in that moment, flowing, melting, and merging. When they realised about the surroundings, they parted. They changed their clothes and sat on a rock under sunlight. The sensations were still deep in both and barely were they able to talk, as if there are some goosebumps in every cell of the body. They dried themselves and, in the meantime, it was a call to move uphill back to the bus. The next destinations were some caves however since sufficient time was already given to the falls and there was some drizzling as well, the tour guide decided to shelve the plan to go to caves and called for a return to Dehradun from there. The group started their trek to the roads uphill. Tara and Avi were walking in the last of the group. Both were silent, as if there were no words to utter. Both were feeling so delicate and fragile, as if they will break if touched. There was so much tingling sensations inside, a different kind of high they were feeling. It was not the usual hormonal gush but much more. As if their souls were drenched and high in love. Silently they were making their way to the up. The trek uphill was little tiring. Everyone was taking rests in between amidst panting and sweating. Avi and Tara were so lost, that they did not even know if they were even tired. They were just walking and stopping only when the whole group was taking a break. There was a mild sprinkle of rain, thankfully, which was keeping the cool somehow.

Their heart was racing fast, and breath were deep. If bench number 594 was emotional high, the falls elevated it at all levels. As if they got much close than ever. Avi felt her fingers tangling with his, he saw her eyes had a shine though half shut. He could feel the hot waves exuding from her tranced face. Tara took him to the sides of stairs, away from the trail of the group, within the green forest plants where they could not be seen. Avi was looking at Tara dumb founded when Tara inched a little closer. She leaned herself a little towards him and as if the soul of Avi knew what this meant. He held her face in his hands, which was like burning hot now. Her trembling lips parted slowly as he touched hers, kissed her. Tara was so much into trance that she just not could open her eyes. Avi paused a little after that, looking at Tara, waiting if he can flow more. Tara did not speak a word, nor she opened her eyes. But her lips, got opened a little like searching for something and her face leaning forward. The soul of Avi understood the language of love, and he flowed along. They kissed each other as if time ceased to exist. Everything else blurred. They were kissing each other so passionately as if somewhere their souls were getting closer. After a while when they came back to their senses, Avi rubbed his nose on her with a smile on his face, holding her face still in his hands. Tara opened her eyes, saw her love Avi, and could not help but smile back with that twinkle in her eyes. Their eyes were wet, wet with love, something they never felt before. She tilted her face when left hand of Avi found its place on her face, and her face then rested on her right shoulder sandwiching his hand between. She pressed her face like this for a while when Avi pulled her close and embraced her. They kept hugging each other for some time while caressing each other's back. Then as if some realisations fell upon them instantly, they parted, and started their journey again to the road. They were walking side by side, holding hands of each other with a smile, as if now it did not matter what the world will think about them. It was open declaration of their love to the world, to the whole cosmos!

They reached their bus. And their journey back to Dehradun started. Tara hailed from Banaras. After the trip she was to take the train today at 10:50 PM. This was the last train to Banaras from Dehradun. She had booked tickets in this as she wanted to have sufficient time plus so much, she wanted to shop locally. Avi wanted Tara to stay for some days, so did Tara. But how much they could stop the time.

They reached Dehradun by 4:00 PM. Avi pursued Tara to stay at Dehradun. He will take her to the places. Will take leaves. "Stay atleast for a day", Avi asked.

"Will come again. You too have office; I too have to attend mine." Tara responded. Avi still kept pursuing her while roaming around the market of paltan bazar near clock tower.

"What do you want to purchase from here?", Avi asked her.

"Nothing as such. Just something which is famous here and some mementos also. I love these small jewelleries and accessories. Though they are available elsewhere as well, even at Banaras, but I just love to shop it from these local markets.", Tara chuckled.

"Take some Butter Pista biscuits from here. There is one old and famous bakery in a gully here which is famous for its mouth-watering biscuits. Take some along. If need be, will send more from here to you", Avi said with all the sincerity on his face.

"You want me to take biscuits from here as souvenirs?", Tara said.

"No! I mean, among other things, do take these. You will love it for sure. Plus, whenever you will have it, remember me", Avi winked while giving a peck on her cheeks.

"Avi, stop it. I don't like PDA," Tara protested as she pushed him away, her cheeks flushing pink. Despite her protests, Avi couldn't keep his eyes off her, orbiting around her with a goofy grin plastered on his face. He had finally found the love of his life, his Tara, and he felt like every love song had been written just for them. She brought him more joy than he had ever experienced before. In that moment, Tara was his everything, the centre of his universe. He silently thanked Shiva for sending her to him from Kashi.

They roamed around a little. Paltan Bazar is quite a huge market with almost everything available within it. Tara purchased some cardigans, winter stoles etc. as she found them quite cheap and quality stuff. They sat at a tea vendor shop to have some fritters with tea. While Tara was enjoying her cup of tea, she realised some sensation on her feet. Avi was doing something on her feet. Wait. What is he doing? Is he wrapping something at my ankles. Is it an anklet?

"Avi!!! What is that? What are you doing?", Tara said in surprised tone.

"You had said, you like these small accessories. I just wanted to give you something which can remind you of me daily. You like blue and green colour, right? That is why I bought these for you. A little bit of green, a little bit of blue on a silver base. Just the way you like it. Like it?", Avi said with deep emotions in his eyes.

"Avi! This is so beautiful. When did you even buy this?"

"When you were bargaining for that cardigan", Avi chuckled.

"Hehe" Tara said. "Bargaining is our birth right", Tara chuckled. "Thank you for this. I loved it". She caressed his cheeks; this gesture touched her heart.

"I also purchased something for you, or us though" she said softly.

"What is that. And when did you purchase it?"

"When I was bargaining on that cardigan", Tara Winked. "Its 8. I am hungry. Let's have something for dinner".

"What would you like to have?" Avi asked gently.

"Tell me the speciality of doon" excitedly she asked.

"Well, Doon is famous for Momos, Chhole Katlambe, Burgers etc. But Momos for dinner, I don't think that would work. There is one famous puri wala at hanuman chowk who serves poori with 4-5 types of Sabjis. It is so mouth-watering, but it opens in the morning and gets closed by early evening. So can't go there. You would like to have some pizza? Ummm! Wait!! Let's go to "the orchards". It serves Thai and Tibetan food, I guess, but the taste and the views from restaurant are mesmerising. Plus, a live band performs as well. What say?" he said like a little boy cracked some big puzzle.

"Your wish my command Sir" she said like a military captain.

As they made their way to the crowded Orchards for dinner, Tara became absorbed in her phone while Avi went to place their order. He watched as she scrolled, feeling a sense of longing for the limited time they had together. 'Tara, can you at least stay with me for these few hours? God knows when we'll see each other again,' he thought to himself. As the minutes ticked by and she remained engrossed in her phone, Avi couldn't help but give her pointed glances.

Eventually, Tara looked up and chuckled at the sight of him. "Just a minute, sweets. Just a minute," she said.

And within a minute itself, Tara was back with him, cooing him and pulling his cheeks. Avi was back to normal again, with her soft gestures. And there they were, together, among the mesmerising views, with some awesome aroma of food, lovely music, and lots of love booming between them. They were constantly looking at each other. At times with words, and other times, the eyes were doing all the talking. After dinner they went out to have ice cream. Their Avi saw a group of Isckon devotees, singing and dancing in group like carrying out a rally. Tara also looked at them and said with a huge smile "Oh! Celebrations of Lord Krishna!".

Avi became curious and like flooded with thousands of questions.

"You taught me how to be in present moment, stillness, enjoying little moments. I did get that but what is this deal about this Hindu culture of worship, devotion etc?" he was confused again and thought, I hope she don't run away with my flood of questions.

"I can answer it. I asked similar question to my dad once since he is also very spiritual and my inspiration. In Bhagwat Gita there are four paths that are mentioned to know ourselves and get free from this cycle. Karam yog or selfless actions, Devotion or bhakti, Jnana yog or knowledge, intellect, and Raja yog or meditation. Following any path with all the sincerity and will, helps in our growth. Like for example, as we flowed in love or merged in nature, the devotees feel the same for their Isht (the God they connect to, may be form or formless), they feel it in every atom, human, animals and flow in love, there is no separation between any living and Isht, they see him or her in all. But that is very high level of devotion like Meera, Surdas, Shri Hit Harivansh, Maha prabhu etc."

"It is similar what I am feeling for you, I can see you everywhere, in everything. Am I doing devotional yog?'. He teased her.

"Yeah! Funny!"

"So, what is your path, Tara?"

"To be honest I am still exploring my path, but I personally feel all paths are important for complete growth and help somehow in this journey. Each of it has own importance" she said.

In this discussion how time came for departure they didn't know. It was already 10.00 P.M. The time for Tara to leave Dehradun was reaching fast and they had to catch the train for Tara at 10:50 PM. Avi looked at Tara, and with an aching heart of near seperation, he started booking cab for station. Tara stopped him in middle. He looked up at Tara, perplexed.

"What happened? You will be late Tara. The train is on...."

"Shhh! I got it cancelled."

"What?? When??", and then he realised where Tara was busy during the dinner. A teardrop rolled down from his eyes and like a contagious disease, it followed in Tara's eyes as well.

"What now?"

"Serendipity"

"Excuse me?"

"I have made booking in a hotel not far from this place. Let us be together, for tonight. Let us flow, with the flow, without thinking about the future or the past. Let us be in the present moment. Let us cherish what we have, rather than thinking about what we can have or could have. What if this is the last day we have? What if there is no tomorrow? Let the time decide for us, and not the vice versa. Let the time decide our time", Tara said.

The moment was one of the most emotional moments of their lifetimes. They checked in to the hotel, went into their room. It was raining outside. Dehradun rains, so unpredictable. This time though, as if the cosmos had planned this rain for them. Like a paradigm, a metaphor, to just flow, to just melt, to just fall, to just be, with each other, for each other, in each other. They sat on seats near window, the rain drops sliding on the window, both looking at each other. A similar rain as if pouring inside them. A strange flow, which never appeared to them. As if today, the blood is flowing differently in the veins, in perfect synchronicity with the rains outside. A raw warmness on the face and the whole body as if they had hours of meditation just before. Nobody remembers who approached the other first. But in minutes, they were in the arms of each other, caressing, cuddling, kissing, exploring, and merging.

As they swayed to the rhythm of an unheard melody, the aroma of rain filled the room. A tune, which only their heart knew. Their eyes were as if in reverie of each other. Avi held her with a gentle, chivalrous embrace as she rested on his chest. She was lying on his arms, half swinging, and he is touching his belly, and sweetness of her countenance. She comes up holding his face in her hands, and they go for the sweetest kiss tasting the nectar of each other. Drinking that nectar of love that tasted no less than any *Amrit*. That taste made them yearn for more, love they never knew even existed. Perhaps a union of two souls in purest of love bathing in each other. Each touch and caress were like making them to crave for more. In the deepest of moments Avi felt like the luckiest man alive in the abyss, he always wanted to make his first love, to his true love and here she is. His Tara, as he tucked away her hairs from her face softly. In that moment he wanted to surrender to her completely at all levels so that nothing remains at the end, who is Tara, who is Avi, don't know but all that remains is love. Same was the state of Tara, she looked at him as she flowed in ecstasy like he is her soulmate, the one she had been looking for. May be this is what Nirvana is, bliss of drowning in ocean of love as they made love. She had tears of love in her eyes which Avi drank, kissed her temple, all she could utter was "Avi, I love you" that bought tears in Avi's eyes as well. "I love you too, my Tara. Never leave me now as I have found answer to my prayers, in you!" and back hugged her as the night dawned.

As Tara tossed and turned in bed that night, she couldn't shake the feeling that she needed to put their love to the test. She wanted to know if Avi was truly her twin flame, a love that would never fade and withstand the passage of time. Even though it was a risky move, her inner voice urged her to follow her heart. However, Tara knew that they both had unfinished business to attend to before they could fully be together. There were still chains holding them back that needed to be broken. With a heavy heart, she scribbled a note for Avi and placed it by his bedside. Tears streamed down her face as she leaned in to kiss his forehead and whispered, "Until we meet again, Avi. Take care of yourself. I'll be waiting for you." Life was strange, she thought, as just a short while ago she was crying tears of joy, and now they were tears of pain.

The sun rose. The beautiful night had ended. Avi woke up alone with a necklace in his neck and a note on the desk.

"Avi. My beautiful and charming Avi. My blessing from cosmos. I could not stay to say goodbye to you, as I would have burst out in tears otherwise. I had no strength to say it in front of you and I know it would have been similar with you. I want to know whether this love is the one or my illusion. Also, I feel we need to work on ourselves, grow, learn lessons, help people, and then re unite after that. We need to find ourselves first and love ourselves to be with each other later. If we are soul partners, no one can change that. We are ought to be together but not now, as this, is not the right time for us. I had felt this before as well, and that is why I called the last night as "Serendipity". I know you don't believe in a lot of things like these, but one day you will. There will be some medium, some thing, which shall help you in finding your own soul calling. Something which shall help you in finding "You". I hope you find it soon Avi and then find me. I won't change my number, nor do you. But we shall never be in touch henceforth unless our paths cross. Let us maintain this, Avi. If the cosmos would want us to be together in this birth, we shall someday. This birth or the next birth or some other I don't know, but we shall walk together this I know. And always remember, this love, what we have, will always be there. No matter what! This cannot change. Never, ever. But we need to walk alone, for our own self and for us. So that we may meet, sooner and walk together. I will wait for you Avi. I will wait for you, my love. I know you will be angry on me for all this, but, trust me, I am doing this for best of us. Come soon love. Grow, expand your horizon, and make this cosmos work for us faster. Whatever I shall do, you will always be there. Goodbye, Love, Tara.

PS: I am leaving one part of pendant with you. It is part of yin yang. This is the gift I had bought for you from that market. Yin completes yang and yang completes yin. They cannot exist differently. The same like us. One part of it (Yang-The light) I am leaving with you, and the other part (Yin-The dark) shall be with me. I hope we match them soon. Much love, my love."

The day had dawned or the dark still continued, Avi could not fathom. He cried the loudest inside the sheets where there was so much love some moments ago.

Chapter 4

Sans Tara

Why you are so far away,
When all you should do is to sway,
Take me in your arms, on your chest I lie,
This is how, I really wanna die..

The pain of distance is heaving sharp,
Nothing soothes, no rains or a harp,
Love is inside, I know that's for sure,
But that warmth of your body, is right now my cure..

Is it already a lifetime, since we met,
When this distance will subside, is all I fret,
I don't want our story to be that of Romeo Juliet,
I want to live with you, and ever after that..

Without you, feel so lonely and sad,
I hope the life after all, will not be so bad,
The sun will shine, where we be together,
Else stop the count of the breaths, can you rather?

Tara's departure left a gaping hole in Avi's life. He was in a shell of his former self, nothing like the person Tara had fallen in love with. He became distant, silent, as if a part of him had been lost forever. She had opened his closed heart, but now he was lost, not knowing what to do or how to move on. It felt like destiny had played a cruel joke on him. Initially, he spent hours pouring over photos of Tara on social media, staring at the yang half of the pendant she had left behind. He wondered why she had left it with him, when she, his light, his yang, his Tara, was gone. He tried to distract himself by working late hours at the office, but the nights were unbearable. He felt numb, as if a part of him had died.

As time passed, Avi began to experience mixed emotions. He was angry and confused, and sometimes he would cry looking at pictures of them together. He found himself questioning whether Tara was right that they had a connection that transcended time and that they were spiritual partners. These thoughts gave him solace, but also left him feeling anguished and in pain. He wondered what the cosmic plan was and if there even was one, or if it was all just something Tara had imagined. He loved Tara deeply, even when he was angry with her for leaving, even when he missed her presence in his life, even when he saw couples in public places. He wanted nothing more than to have her back in his life, but she was gone, like a star that had disappeared from the sky without a trace, truly giving meaning to her name, "Tara."

Two years passed; Tara was gone, long gone. The life had so called came on track again. He had started smiling but it was mostly on surface and little from his heart. The more of a corporate smile than a real one. He had got promoted to a senior level. Finances were right, owned a car and a house. One thing still missing, Tara. He missed her, still! The frequency of cries had brought down significantly, which was like a daily routine with a loud cry earlier, had now transformed into occasional tears like rolling of teardrops once in blue moon. One thing which remained constant though was to see her pictures daily, and yang pendant mostly at the time of bed. Moved on but just could not move on! He knew how to roll on from a normal crush or attraction or even first love he had in college. But this, how to move on from someone who touched your heart, stirred your soul became a part of your existence!

Most of his friends were getting married. Some even had children. His own family was pressing hard on him to get married but how could he? What about the serendipity? What about Tara. Where the heck is she. Why she is not coming back to my life. Why are our paths not getting crossed? And will it ever? This nation, which has second highest number of populations in the world, of more than 130 crores people, is it possible that the two of them would meet, ever?

These questions were troubling him hard. He was not able to get out of it. The societal expectations, family pressures were taking enough toll on him. His parents were religiously finding a suitable match for him and were sending matrimonial profiles for him to select. Nobody wanted to understand his reluctance, and everyone was taking his resentment as his unwillingness to get married at present. "Marriage" he never actually understood this concept fully. It was like some crazy herd mentality induced in society and some reasons families put across don't even make any sense.

His parents were constantly nagging him to get married, citing the fact that his friends and cousins were all settling down and that he was getting older. They talked about their desire to see him with children, and the pressure of what society would say if he remained single. He wanted to retort, "What if it doesn't work out and my life becomes even more tumultuous after marriage? What if the partner isn't right and all the little peace I have is replaced with stress, fights, and toxicity? Will you and society still support me if I want to get out of it?" But as usual, he couldn't voice these thoughts. He knew that their pressure for him to get married had nothing to do with true happiness, peace, or love, and that it was just about fulfilling societal expectations. He knew that he would only settle down with someone like Tara, his soulmate, otherwise what was the point in getting married?

"When is the right time to get married then?", His mom asked in typical tone one day.

'I don't know. I just know that I am not ready at this juncture" he said sternly.

"What do you mean this juncture?"

"My career is on priority. There are lot of other things I must deal. I just cannot marry some random girl. I need to know a person first then only I can think of marrying someone. This arrange marriage concept is beyond my understanding." He tried to explain.

"FYI, me and your dad got married with this concept itself".

"Yeah, I know. And how beautiful is your marriage that too I know" he said sarcastically.

"This comment was irrelevant".

"Whatever, please!!! I don't want to peruse it. I need time. I cannot get married to someone just like that after having evening snacks at our's or her home or some restaurant with tea and giving shagun on that day itself like, some task got completed. चलो जी रोका हो गया | बधाई हो | Like seriously no! That is not my idea of marriage. You never understood and supported me in any aspect of life and always forced your dreams on me, I am a human being with my own dreams as well and not a puppet" he couldn't control anymore and exploded.

She got silent for a bit and then asked, "Then what is your idea of marriage?"

"To me, the marriage is a union of two people or rather union of two souls and..." He could not complete the sentence. The word "soul" again took him back to the memories of Tara. "Soul partners".

"Avi, we're not saying you have to get married right away after meeting someone. Take your time, we're not forcing you. But at least start putting yourself out there, start dating. Meet new people and see if you have common interests or anything that you like. Take time to get to know them, but at least make an effort to start talking to people and seeing who a good fit for you as a life partner might be. It might take days, weeks, or months to figure it out, but you never know where or how you'll meet the right person. Just start somewhere, at least".

His mom and her dominating way of stimulating things in her own way. There was no point explaining her that marriage is not equally proportional to so called happiness.

"Okay. Give me a month and then send me those profiles." He just wanted to get rid of this conversation.

"Why a month?"

"Mom!!!" he was ready to detonate again.

"Okay. Take this time but be sure that after that you will start seeing the profiles, we shall send you. Or you yourself can also check the profiles. There is this mobile app also for this matchmaking website, download it in your phone and see it on your own. Your dad has already created your profile".

"Yeah, yeah" he brushed off.

"But what will you do?" His mother asked again without paying heed to previous ferocious reply of Avi. Avi knew there is no escape to this. His mother will not stop until he tells her.

"I want to go on a solo trip".

"What? Where? Why? Take us along!"

"No! Solo trip means to go alone if you can understand that."

"Yeah, I understand. But why solo. नवे नवे fashion चला रखे आजकल दे मुंडेया ने|" she poked.

"I just want to listen to my inner voice. Like what I want from this life now. How I see it and how I want to see it. And I want to be in nature, becoming one with it. Want that peace badly. With family, that is not possible. Plus, I don't want to spoil my holiday by constantly being nagged about aloo de paranthe, maggiya, paneer di sabji, look at that girl wearing so short dresses, this auto wala looted us with two extra pennies, Hotel rooms were not clean, they did not give us extra tea sachets, Tea was not tasty, these people don't treat tourist well, etc. etc."

"Huh!"

"Thank you"

Avi felt lost and aimless, unsure of what he wanted from life. He knew that he needed a change of scenery, a solo trip to clear his mind and find some answers. He hoped that the trip might also serve as a sign from the universe about Tara and their relationship. Maybe they would cross paths again, if they were meant to be, or maybe it would be a sign for him to let go and move on. He wanted to find a place of serenity and peace, a place where he could find himself again.

He decided to take a trip from Ahmedabad where he had just been transferred for a promotion. He spread out a map and began to consider his options. After some time, he pinpointed a few locations, including a hill range that called to him in a strange, inexplicable way. He picked Mount Abu, Mandsaur and Goa, planning to spend two days at Mount Abu, one day at Mandsaur and the rest of the time exploring Goa. He would spend around 70 hours on the road, traveling and the rest of the time would be for visiting places and rest. He took some time off from work and packed his bags with food supplies, granola bars, and other necessities like sheets, a comforter, and pillows. Next morning, He woke up fully rested and set out for his journey, ready for the adventure ahead.

The journey started well in time. He reached Mount Abu in 4 hours. Went on to see Dilwara Temples, which are old Jain Temples. He found a lot of good spiritual energies there, where he tried to stay in meditation for some time. There were some segments in the temples which were booming with such high energies which Avi could feel a lot. After spending some good time there, he went to see famous Nakki Lake. He spent the evening in the solace of lake, did some boating and watched birds. He was feeling light. He had not taken a break since the time Tara had left him. He so wanted this break to rejuvenate. There is a garden near to the lake, where he sat for a longer time. He saw people passing by. Smiled at some, helped some. He wrote a poem there, a lost passion of his which was as if again rekindled.

Was walking by a road,
A bit slow and had a load,
Reached a garden, famous though,
Found myself a bench and poised my toe.
Lots of people here and there,
Choc a bloc the garden with peculiar affair,
Felt uncomfortable, strolled myself again,
Saw a boy with a smiling chain.
Laughing and clapping weirdly haired,
time to realise, he is physically impaired,
was carrying a small roller coaster board,
though it was not meant for any sport.
Tried to realise the reason for smile,
saw a bunch of boys playing away while,
He was happy on the joy he never owed,
That turning and twisting of his board.
A happy boy, sweet boy of a pauper clan,
was still much richer than his spectator man,
restarted my journey on garden's tile,
Had one more thing, a contagious smile.

The day was nice, after so long, he felt some happiness inside. He was quite tired from the journey as well the busy day, so he retired to bed in no time.

The next day, he visited Arbuda Devi Temple (Adhar Devi). It is a small temple situated on a hill amidst lustrous greenery. When he reached there it started to drizzle, he felt like those drops are cleaning him as well from inside. The temple has around 365 steps, like reminding a step for each day of a year. He was trying to be in that moment and connect with nature. He reached the temple, which was on top, a temple of Arbuda Devi, a reincarnation of Katyayani Devi, a form of Mother Shakti as believed. When he entered the cave, he felt beautiful loving energies. He saw the face of Devi ji, and he felt as if she is blessing him with so much love and affection. As if she is the Goddess of compassion. He sat there for a while, closed his eyes and like heard a whisper "My child come and rest in my laps, a tough journey waits for you", as he opened the eyes he felt tears in them, even he didn't know how. He felt so light after that like a son feels in his mother's lap. He then went to an adjoining terrace with the temple, as he entered there, he gasped his breath watching such a beauty, whole trail of Mount Abu was visible from there.

The next day he started his journey to Daman which was his intermittent stop before Goa. He reached Daman in lunch time and strolled at Jampore Beach. The climate was windy that day and the air was cool. He spent time there relaxing and explored some local cuisines. Next day, He left early in the morning. That is the best about solo trips, the time we get with ourselves without any distraction and disturbances, except the mind of course and its convos. Here it started again,

"Hey Buddy," said the mind.

"Who are You?" Avi asked.

"I am your mind. Hello!"

"What do you want?"

"I just want your good. There is no point of being so pessimistic in life. Go ahead. Find someone else".

"Crude! I don't need your advice. I will follow my heart".

"Your heart? Haha! It will keep guiding you wrong, as usual. It wants you to be diving deep into slumbers. Into the shackles of misery and loneliness. Without love. Come to terms Avi, she never intended to come back to your life. Who on earth would say this stupid serendipity thing? She wanted an excuse to be away from you. She must have moved on by now, settled down, doing well in her career, and here you are. Silly drowned man. Still waiting for some miracle that woof, and here comes Tara. Slow Claps!!"

"Shut up!!!"

"You can try to shut me up, bro, but listen. My job is to tell you the naked truth that you've been ignoring so far. I don't want you to see the world through rose-colored glasses. Be practical! You know the chances of you seeing her again in this lifetime are next to impossible, unless the majority of the population gets wiped out in some apocalypse and the two of you survive to save the world, like in some pulp fiction."

(Silence)

"Look, Avi! The chapter of Tara is closed. Accept this and move on. Open your arms to the future and let go of the past. If she was going to come back, she would have by now. Just imagine, after 10 years, even if she doesn't come back and you're still stuck in the past, will it be fair to you, your spouse, and kids, if any, and your parents? Let her go.

There are some people who come and go, only a few remain with us for a longer time. Think of the beautiful future instead of dwelling on the past. If you remain occupied in the past, you'll never be able to welcome the future. The choice is yours!"

The mind had done its job. It played and played well. Avi was under total control and spell of what his mind had said. Avi thought a lot about it and found that his mind was right. It was time to move on, indeed. With a heavy heart, he saw her display picture for the last time and deleted her contact and all the photos he had of her. He unfriended her on social media profiles, even though Tara had never been active on those. Maybe this would help him to explore other potential partners now.

After an arduous long journey, he reached Goa in the evening. "Goa" what a beauty it is, like ready to offer whatever one desires for, party or serenity. The whole journey was breath-taking one with some spectacular roadside views, some villages he passed by, had local food and booze in some local eateries. Mount Abu had given him a kickstart and somehow Goa gave him the actual kick. He felt so much jolliness and that long lost kid inside him somehow was coming up again. He went to a nearby café for his breakfast and a famous shack to drink. One day in café he was sipping his latte when a girl came to him and asked.

"I hope you would not mind if I joined you" she smiled. He noticed that he has been seeing this girl from two days as he started to visit this café. Maybe she was a regular customer there. She was beautiful with a chic appeal. Her eyes were very bright, twinkling with an unknown mystery. She was quite attractive, and he was curious about her.

"Please, the pleasure is all mine," he replied in a charming tone.

"Thanks, so what brings you to Goa?" she inquired.

"I'm here on a solo trip, trying to rediscover myself and, of course, to enjoy the parties and the tranquillity of the place," he said cheerfully.

"You are quite an interesting combination of a human, I must say," Meera said, and they both laughed.

"What brings you here?" he asked in return.

"I'm something of an explorer, I love water sports and connecting with like-minded people," Meera replied excitedly.

"That sounds quite interesting, Ms. Explorer," he teased.

"So, what are your plans for today?" she asked.

"Not much, really. Any suggestions?" he asked.

"Come join me. Let's go for some water sports and then head to a nearby shack party. I know some people there," she said playfully.

"Sounds like a plan! But before we go, may I ask for your name?" he was curious.

"You're quick to ask, aren't you? My name is Meera, and yours?" she asked in return. "Avi"

They painted the town red, surfing, snorkelling, para gliding, giggling, exploring goa like never before. Avi was certainly attracted to her easy-going fun vibe, something he was certainly lacking since a long time. Though she had something more to her, a wise streak she was perhaps hiding for now.

As they cruised down the winding road, the sound of a classic 90's tune of 'wo pehli baar jab hum mile' filled the car. Suddenly, she turned down the volume and asked, "Avi, how do you define Love?"

He paused for a moment to collect his thoughts before answering. "Love can not be bound in definitions. It's a state of being where boundaries and definitions cease to exist. The word 'definition' literally means to define, to determine, to demarcate something. But how to put demarcation on something which is free by its very nature?"

He continued, "Love is something where the finite becomes infinite, and form becomes formless. In love, there is no separation between anything or anyone - not between God, humans, or even living and non-living things. All becomes one, and one becomes all. Love is a feeling that touches your soul as if a river flowing through your heart and sweeping you away. It is as pure as divine! It's something that even poets, sufis, and writers struggle to put into words. That my dear love is to me."

She was spellbound, "You suddenly reminded me of Rumi and Shamz".

"Seriously, you like them? I knew you have so much more to you". Avi was more attracted to her now.

"Yes, their one quote", she looked deeply in his eyes and said "Love cannot be explained. It can only be experienced. Love cannot be explained, yet it explains all".

In evening they went to an evening shack party. "Do you dance?" Meera asked Avi.

"Yes Meera, I would love to dance with you", they slowly swirled on an English number "Strangers in the night by Frank Sinatra" that was playing in the background.

Strangers in the night

Exchanging glances

Wond'ring in the night

What were the chances

We'd be sharing love

Before the night was through?

Something in your eyes was so inviting

Something in your smile was so exciting

Something in my heart told me

I must have you

Strangers in the night

Two lonely people

We were strangers in the night

Up to the moment

When we said our first hello

Little did we know

Love was just a glance away

A warm embracing dance away

They were looking in each other eyes, sparks were flying, slowly when they came together and kissed, they didn't know, but suddenly, as they were kissing, a flash of Tara came in Avi's mind, and he pulled back.

"What happened Avi?"

"Ahh nothing" he brushed off like nothing happened and tried to change the awkward vibe, "You want to drink more? let me bring for you". He came back and while drinking he looked at the sunset and whispered slowly in her ears "How beautiful the sun set is, let's go for a walk".

"Sure, even I want to go somewhere quiet, too noisy here".

They went for a stroll and settled down somewhere deserted on the beach. He touched her fingers slowly and held her hands, they came close again, this time diving more into each other, giving way to intense moments of love. As they were on verge of final moments, Avi said slowly "I love you Tara".

"Tara!! What's wrong with you Avi? I am Meera!" She snapped at him.

"I am sorry, I just zoned off" he looked down as he couldn't face her.

"I genuinely liked you, to be honest, I even felt we could have so much more than a normal fling, I liked that depth in your vibe, but you seem to be a wounded man with a broken heart that is still unhealed. You should have not given me the signs if you weren't ready. This is so not cool".

"I am sorry Meera, I genuinely am, can we give this another chance? I really connected with you well and had so much fun with you" he was disappointed in his own self, seriously what is wrong with him.

"I don't think so Avi, going ahead with you will be like a path to hurt myself more because I know I will fall for you and get hurt because you are broken inside. I am not ready for such connect. I really had time of my life with you, but this should end now. A last piece of advice I want to give you, either go get that girl or completely move on and give yourself another chance. You can't stay like this forever!" and she left.

It was like somebody slapped him to come into his senses. He kept sitting there, staring at the waves washing ashore, it was like a déjà vu for him, years before he was in quite similar position to attract love of his love but this time, he was here to bid her final adieu in some way so that he can move onto next phase of his life. He looked at the yang pendant and whispered to those waves " Oh' dear sea, the core of you is water which is everywhere, please be my messenger and give this message to her, Tara I hope you are doing well, I don't even know whether you remember me or not but thank you for coming in my life turning my life upside down at all levels. I really missed you and a part of me will always belong to you but for now it is time to let you go. I am done waiting now and this whole serendipity thing, Goodbye Tara" He whispered with tears in his eyes for one final time for her, but he had kind of a closure of it now.

Previously he had thought to stay at Mumbai while return but then he thought it would be better to stay at Nashik than Mumbai as Mumbai he had already seen plus, he wanted to visit Tryambakeshwar Temple. It is a Shiva Temple and one of the twelve Jyotirlingas. There was a huge rush in the temple but somehow, he could visit it. Felt the vibes, stayed there for some time, had a smile as he connected a lot with Shiva. He was sitting in the stairs outside in the temple campus where one monk came across. He saw Avi, smiled at him incessantly. He was wearing an orange upper wear and a dhoti draped in the bottom with a white head gear. He closed his eyes and put his hand on Avi's head and then left after some time. Avi saw him going like dumbstruck. Who was he? He stood up to leave when suddenly something fell off from his head. It was a flower, an orange-coloured flower. He took it in his hands and felt as if he got connected to some electricity source. His eyes got closed and felt that trance. He kept that flower in his pocket and came out of the premises. He spent that night in Nashik.

Next day, he got woke up suddenly early in the morning. He saw his phone to check the time. It was 5:55 AM. He started his journey for Mandsaur, in Madhya Pradesh after breakfast at hotel. Mandsaur was on his list as he had got a dream of Pashupati Nath Ji a day before he thought of this travel. Though when he thought about Pashupati Nath ji, he went on to think about the famous Nepal temple. But when he started searching for it, he found out that there is one temple in India as well at Mandsaur. And that is how Mandsaur became part of his travel list.

He came to Mandsaur in evening and when he reached temple, he checked his watch, it was 5:55 PM. He deposited his shoes at the shoe counter before entering the temple, and got token, token number 555 so that he can recollect his shoes later.

As soon as Avi entered the temple, he felt a sense of familiarity wash over him, an emotional response he had never experienced before. Despite not understanding why, tears welled in his eyes and a smile spread across his face. He felt as if he had come home after a long journey, like he belonged there. He felt as if he was being welcomed by a host of deities, being showered with blessings and flowers. He couldn't understand the visions that he was experiencing, or why he was experiencing sudden, sharp pain in the center of his forehead, like what he felt the day Tara helped him balance his third eye chakra.

As he joined the line to enter the *garbhagriha*, the energy in the temple intensified. Everyone was chanting "Om Namah Shivay" and the sound of bells filled the temple. He felt an overwhelming sense of spiritual elevation, and his attention was fully absorbed by the eight-faced Shiva linga as soon as he entered the garbhagriha. It was an eight-faced linga with four faces on top in a line, and other four faces just below them, again in a line. As he approached the linga, he stumbled and was caught by a fellow visitor. He couldn't see anything or anyone else, all he could see was the linga. He felt like the smiling face of one of the faces welcomed him with open arms. Avi entered with the crowd and was out as quickly, He was left standing in front of the river Shivna, perplexed and unsure of what had just occurred. He was talking to himself without paying attention to people around him.

"What was that? What is this rush of energy? Why am I feeling this, Trance? What is the story of this linga? Why am I crying for no reason like a baby? Why I am no more in control of my body?" He composed himself and sat at a bench nearby for some time. After attaining back his senses, he went to that open area where Nandi Ji was there. He sat near to him. The Linga was totally visible from this place as the rush had settled now. He doesn't know what happened, but his eyes got closed automatically. And as if he was being pushed to some other world, he went into a deep meditative state.

"What is this? A fire? Ohh!! It's a bon fire. There are people dancing around it. Are these humans or animals? Animals, no humans. Wait! There are animals and one human. No! He is not human. He is part human. Face of a tiger and body of a human. What is he and these animals doing? And what is this in the centre? Wait.. Is it? Is it, the Linga!!!" Avi opened his eyes in an instant. He could not understand what he saw. Was it some kind of vision like once Tara had. He felt dizzy, nothing was making sense. What on the Earth was happening to him. Suddenly, He tilted his head and saw a flex banner which read, "Shiv Bhandara for needy for continuous 555 days".

He stood up, somehow, gaining his consciousness still in utter confusion to what he saw. He was going out of temple, when somebody stopped him and said, 'Brother, you can take *prasadam* from that counter'. He was in no senses, was in full trance, he just followed what that fellow man said to him. He went to counter, took some prasadam. The counter man gave him receipt. His eyes were blurry and all he could see was the receipt number, which showed, Sl. No. 555.

He somehow strolled himself back to the hotel, and for the first time in past two years, went to sleep without having any food, booze, or smokes.

Next day, he woke up late in the morning. His head was still heavy from the last day's affair. He sat upright and started processing things. He could not understand a thing about what he saw in the visions he got while meditating in the temple. It was quite late, he called at reception to check whether they are still serving the breakfast buffet. Luckily, they were. He locked his room which was on fifth floor, in that trance state and went on roof top restaurant on Ninth Floor, to have his breakfast. His head was so heavy and tipsy, he immediately had a cup of tea then had some things to eat. When suddenly like something clicked inside him and a realisation happened.

As Avi settled himself into a seat with his breakfast and cup of tea, he could not shake the feeling that something was different. He noticed that the room number was 555, the same as the receipt he received at the temple earlier that day, and the time he arrived at the temple was 5:55 PM. To top it off, even the token number at the shoe counter was 555. He couldn't shake the feeling that this was more than just a coincidence. He decided to look it up online and when he did, the first thing that came up was a 555-timer integrated circuit, but he ignored it as he was not interested in science. But then one of the results caught his eye, it was "Angel Number 555".

He started reading about it. He got to know that angel numbers are a pattern of numbers we see often at some point of our life, which is a message from our guardian angel. They try to connect to us through numbers and we see a distinct pattern of numbers which has a peculiar meaning attached to it. Like he was seeing 555.

He was taken aback when he read some 5-6 articles on it. 555 particularly was talking about a paradigm shift in life, major changes, and transformation. And that during this transition, the guardian angels shall assist him in his life path to go through these changes, smoothly. The guidance will be passed on by the angels, higher selves, divine selves etc., so that the person can sail through this course of transformation. "Higher self! Divine Self! Tara had spoken about it. She had also seen ours!"

"But what transformation is waiting for me? What kind of change? Shiva, O lord, please guide me. What should I do!! I heard this message through angels or whatever. But what am I gonna do now? Tell me, Shiva!! In Goa on the beach after the incidence with Meera I have now let go of Tara, I know she won't come, and this serendipity is all crap. Now all these signs seem to be a clear indication I must enter a new phase of life but still my heart is not able to. At this point in life, when I don't know what I need from my life and what am I doing with it, where my parents are so behind me to get married, tell me what am I supposed to do? I had planned this trip to get answers. Rather, I have more questions now than ever. My life is already stuck up. What change? I am single, do you want me to..."

"Can I sit beside you?" suddenly he saw an old man came there to have a cup of tea. He looked like a man in his fifties, his hairs had greyed, and he looked like a tourist who came to visit the temple. One that really caught Avi attention was his eyes, his soft yet piercing strong gaze.

"Yes, why not, you came to eat alone?"

"You seemed to be lost in some deep thought son, something seems to be troubling you" as he sipped his tea.

"Oh! well nothing, you also came here to visit Pashupati Nath Ji?" he asked.

"Yes son, I feel a strong connection with him. I am an old man now what else is left to do in life than visit temples" and he started to laugh. "But what brings you here?"

"Oh, nothing really just exploring different places and happened to come here," he said casually.

"Nothing happens just like that; everything happens for a reason. Just when we think life is not turning out to be the way we wanted and feel we are stuck, rather than fighting or resisting it we can try to accept things and circumstances as they are, who knows all the answers lies in that surrender and acceptance. And maybe that is what this form of Pashupath Nath Ji all about, taming your inner beast and surrendering it to him. Okay son, time for me to go, my family is waiting for me downstairs, by the way it was a strong cup of tea" he winked and smiled and just like that disappeared.

Avi was just mum; he couldn't utter a single word. It felt like the universe sent answers to all his questions through him. He was grateful to lord Shiva, and silently he geared up for a new beginning to his life, dark or light that time will tell but whatever it will be he had to trust and put faith now.

For the last time, he looked at the yang pendant, shed the last drop of tear and texted his mom, the very minute. "Mumma. I am ready to get married!"

Chapter 5

Marriage

Life is a long journey, companionship is the way,

Red threads of attachment or match made in heaven, as they say,

Love is all about freedom, and not the other way,

If a station binds your legs, better not to stay!

Considering it to be God's sermon, Avi agreed to get married. His parents of course were very happy for him. They flooded his inbox with umpteen number of profiles. Some of them belonged to same profession, some same caste, some same city where now they were living, some had all the above or some "qualities", et cetera. He started meeting girls, as suggested by his parents. With most of the girls he could not connect. May be at back of his mind somehow, he compared everyone to Tara. And since there was no another Tara, he mostly never liked any girl. He met a dozen of girls, mostly at cafes or at times the whole family used to go to the girl's home. He was like tired now. He was seeking a deep soul connection, if not similar yet at least close to what he had with Tara. But what he was feeling was very surface level materialistic approach to this whole institution of marriage. Like for the sake of society, family we are bound to bind ourselves with someone or else fears are incorporated. "How will you live alone your life?" 'You need someone to take care in old age' 'You don't think and care about our reputation in society'. Avi still couldn't understand this whole so called marriage thing if it's not your soulmate. The one who can stir your whole existence with just one single glare of eyes. The one whose simple touch can send goosebumps to each cell of your body. The one who not only help you grow, heal at emotional but also at spiritual level. The one who helps you question yourself and support in becoming a better version of your own self. He had felt all this with Tara in that short time, and what a heavenly fairy tale it could be to have her as his wife. But destiny always have other plans, he couldn't understand that then. Perhaps Avi was not ready for this heavenly deep union with Tara and had to undergo series of tests and lessons. He was prepping himself to let go Tara and enter new chapter, but perhaps he was taking one step further towards her. Universe works in mysterious ways if so, only we can understand the complete picture. One day his mom came to his room.

"Avi. You remember Nimmi Aunty from Agra?"

"The one who is your distant cousin and is half wise?"

"Shut up! Yeah, the same. She had called just now. They know one family through one of their friends in Agra itself. The family is nice, well to do. They are a nuclear family of four. The father is into business and their daughter is an MBA from some good college. She is working for some MNC, Nimmi had told me the name, I forgot. They are co incidentally here at Ahmedabad on some personal trip. Nimmi had sent your profile to them, and they have liked you. I also saw her photos and she look nice to me. Her name is Malvika. They have shown their interest to meet us. They are here till tomorrow. I can ask them to come at our home for lunch and evening tea. You guys can meet and talk, spend some time together and see if it works. What say?"

"Hmmm. Okay."

Avi's mom called them and requested them to come to their home. They graciously agreed. They too wanted to find a suitable match for their girl. In no time their family was at Avi's home, around mid-day. The families got engaged in talking, where their dads started talking about politics & cricket and moms about customs and traditions of their families and how it was different in their maternal houses from here. Siblings were talking about latest games, memes, YouTube channels and Insta reels and Avi & Malvika soon were cornered, intentionally by some and unintentionally by others. They both knew why they were meeting and as usual, the shyness and hesitation was evident. After a time, it went quite awkward and then Avi came with an ice breaker.

"So, you are here at Ahmedabad for some wedding to attend, I suppose" he asked.

"Yeah. My distant cousin's wedding it is for which we are here." She replied with bit shyness.

"Okay. And how did you find this place?" he enquired?

"Nice", Malvika said it with a smile, taking some strands of her hairs falling onto her face to back of her ears.

Avi came directly to the point. "See. You have seen my profile and I have seen yours. We know basic things about each other and let us not waste our time on that. I want to ask you two pertinent things straight. First, why you want to get married? And if you do want to get married, why you want to consider me?"

Malvika took a moment to process the direct tone of question posed at her. She tried finding her composure and replied, "Imagine yourself, stranded on an island, alone, for four years like what happens to that character in that movie "Cast Away". Forget about four years, you won't be able to survive for some months. It would be so painful to live a solitary life there. You remember what that character Tom Hanks had played had done there? He used one volleyball and named him Wilson. He talked to him throughout that time he was on that island like he was a real human. And how he had cried when he got separated from him in the middle of his journey from that island back to home. As if he lost his friend, his mate in actual. Even when it was just a volleyball but for him, he was everything!!

Life is a long journey. Human beings are people centric. We need people to get going. Some we need for our temporary needs, like friends, acquaintances, colleagues who are like passers-by with whom we derive temporary affection and strength to move ahead. Then there are some who are or who become our foundations like solid pillars of our life from which we derive our true happiness, love, joy, and those emotions which we can't show or share with everyone. These are our special people and one of those special people in our life is our partner, to whom we get married. Who is even more special than others as we share almost every little thing with that person which we don't even share with our parents who gave us birth. There are times when we are happy, and we want to share it with that special person to expand our happiness, feel that happiness better and then there are times when we are not happy, sad, emotionally low and we need that solid permanent shoulder to cry on, to get embraced when we are down, so that we can stand again to face the world heads on. Everybody thinks of her prince charming or his princess with whom he or she wants to spend the rest of their life. Like they say in Bollywood, happily ever after. I do want that special person in my life with whom I can spend my life growing together, taking care of each other, and becoming a strength of each other.

I have met a lot of people in my life, during my education and now in this job. Mostly, I could not feel any deep connection with them and, especially, I never could feel that *thing*, I don't know what to call it, but you can say like mirror to our own feelings or something like that. I could never see that or feel that in anyone's eyes yet except today when I saw yours. Your eyes have that honesty, that charm, that calm, and your eyes speak it all. And the best part is, it travels. It is so effortlessly travelling to me, and I can feel these vibes. I could never see myself better or could felt that warmth that I am feeling since I met you. That is one of the reasons why I was very silent throughout as I was not being able to comprehend what it is. I don't know what shall happen after this meeting but surely, I would love to be in touch with you always, even if you chose to not get married to me."

Avi listened to it all. After Tara, she was the only girl who praised him, made some logical sense, as anyways he was so much into his shell lately. Though his heart was not beating for her, in that way, but he was flattered by what she spoke. And he saw a twinkle in her eyes for him. He was able to feel that she indeed had found great endearment for him and could feel her inclination towards him. And surprisingly, this was just the first meeting of theirs!

"Was my response not proper?" Malvika asked little surprised as Avi had gone silent afterwards.

"No! It's not that. I was just lost in something, excuse me for that." Avi returned with a smile.

They talked about many things. They connected well, though Avi could not get that feeling for her, not even close to what he had for Tara. But the way she mingled up with his parents, how she became instant favourite of all the children in his house, and the way she looked at Avi with so much of fondness and kind of care, he felt happy about it. In some way or the other, everyone liked her presence in the house. So did Avi. Everyone was happy, everyone was smiling, laughing, and this is what Avi always wanted. Happy family! Someone who can connect this not so connected family. Moreover, she can be the rebound now he desperately seeked so did his broken heart.

It was getting dusky outside. Family of Malvika had to leave as they had a flight to catch way back home. Though Avi's mom tried her best that they stay at Ahmedabad a day more, more out of courtesy than anything else, but since everyone had work to catch so one more day was not at all feasible especially as it was not planned earlier. The whole family came out to see them off. Everyone connected nicely and somehow both their parents could feel that Malvika and Avi too went along well. It was all evident in the body language. The cab arrived, Malvika's family got seated after sharing hugs and all with each other. Avi touched the feet of Malvika's parents as per traditions and looked at her father with smile on his face. Her father held him with his shoulders with a broad smile and hugged him for few moments. Her mother too showered her blessings on him when he touched her's. Avi looked at Malvika who had by now seated in the cab with her family and waved hand to say bye. Malvika returned the wave with a sweet smile and the cab cranked up the speed and was gone in no seconds.

His mom was staring at him with a mischievous smile as if she knew what happened. Moms!! How do they know things so well? How can they comprehend, especially these scenarios, so well.

"So! How was it?" with the same mischievous smile she asked Avi.

"Mom! It's just a single meeting. Give her some time and to me as well. Can you?" Avi retorted.

"Yeah, take your time. I am just asking how it went. And could you relate with her? I liked the girl, being honest", His mom was not just mischievous but was pestering as well.

"You like every girl under the sun".

"Avi!!!"

"She was nice mom. I felt good talking to her. Don't know how it shall culminate in future but yeah had a good conversation with her. And that is enough for you to know as you are now entering into my personal space. Move a little!!!"

"Okay! I got what I wanted to hear" And his mom went away leaving him alone in his room smiling all the way.

He spent some time tossing on his bed thinking of what all happened. He had a smile on his face throughout, a short but warm smile. Usually, he listened to some music before going to bed, tonight he was in mood to listen to sweet melody of flute and Tabla. As his consciousness started to dwell deeper into the tones becoming one with it suddenly, he started to feel bit uneasy. Like a presence of someone showing him something. He was shown a vision of some misty grey clouds hovering over him. And slowly he drifted off to sleep. He had a dream that night. He saw himself walking on a beautiful road surrounded with trees and meadows. After a while he saw two paths ahead of him, one was like a deserted road with lots of obstacles, darkness, but saw all his family members there smiling at him including Malvika who was wearing a beautiful black gown smiling at him. On that road he felt destination is very near. While on the other road though there was no darkness or obstacles but also no greenery there, yet it was bit lonely and felt destination is too far. This dream jolted him up, he was like sweating profusely. He couldn't understand the meaning of this dream but had a knack that he was at Criss cross, and an important choice had to be made by him. Due to lack of awareness and being blinded by emotional attachments he decoded it by thinking his family and Malvika are the ones who will help and support him in reaching his destination. His companions and well-wishers for life who will be with him thick and thin no matter how dark it gets or obstacles come. He felt it is like the universe signalling him to choose that path that is what his destiny is. Well, he was right, it was his destiny to choose that path as that would bring him inch closer to his destination. The question was those he saw on that dark path will be his saviours or actually the pushers.

Ignorant of any such hunch, after a while he reached out to see the time on his watch. Malvika's flight was to take off in 15-20 minutes. He reached to his phone and texted her.

"Best of Journey. It was nice meeting.", with a smiley emoji.

"Thanks. It indeed was a nice meeting", Malvika returned in no time with the same emoji he used.

"Is the Flight on time? Have you boarded?"

"Yes. We have. Just about to fly in few minutes"

"Okay, Great. Safe Journey. Take care of yours."

"Thanks once again Avi. You too take good care of yours."

He plugged his phone into charging and went on to have dinner. His mom had another energy and mood. She was so happy as her son had met a girl and had a good connect with her. She was already dreaming about their wedding, how she will call her "Daughter in law", what arrangements she needs to make in Avi's room, new furniture to replace the old ones, guests list, venue for wedding, who will give how much "shagun", pandit who will do all the rituals, name of their kids, and what not. She was flying high in some fairy land as if she was high on poppies. Though, her radiant energy was working only for day dreaming and not for the other things like food, as nothing she prepared for the dinner since there was too much left over from the lunch and evening snacks and as a prudent Punjabi mom, she mixed it all and made "Gatava", a Punjabi delicacy, which Punjabi moms make when they are in no mood to cook and there is lot of food in the refrigerator which they dint intend to throw away or give it to the dogs as it was just at max 3 days old. So instead of giving it to dogs, it is given to a better breed, "The Family".

He watched some reality shows on TV and had some chatter with the family while dinner. He came back to his room after finishing his dinner and took out a book he was reading these days. He read a page or two and then he remembered he had plugged his phone for charging. He took his phone out and saw one text notification. It read, "Landed just about now. Throughout this flight I was thinking about you only and a short and sweet smile has not left me since the time we met. I don't know what you are feeling now, but this feeling is beautiful what I am feeling inside of me. Thanks."

Avi ended the conversation with a smiley face and a "Take Care" message. He wasn't sure what to say next. That night, he was feeling a mix of emotions. On one hand, he had enjoyed his meeting with Malvika. It had been nice and friendly, and he had felt comfortable opening to someone again. On the other hand, there was Tara. She was his love, his soulmate. He was still struggling with his feelings. His heart was telling him that this might not be what he truly wanted. He kept asking himself, "Is Malvika really someone I can see myself spending my life with?"

Three hours in bed, and he was still tossing and turning. Not getting what to do. His head was so heavy with all these talks about Malvika and Tara and the dream. Was he decoding the dream right, was she really the one. As he thought about Malvika it used to be almost like someone pushing him, go for it. He remembered her smiling face from the dream like telling him, I will do anything for you Avi just come to me. He stood up and went to the refrigerator to get himself a bottle of water. In the mid-way, back to his room, he heard voices from his parents' room. They were talking about Malvika and her family. They were really happy meeting her and her family. Everyone was like having a dream of his marriage, except of course him. He quietly opened the door to his parents' room, making sure they wouldn't notice. He watched them, their faces alight with happiness. It had been a while since he had seen them so content. One meeting had brought so much joy to their lives. He thought about how he could keep that happiness on their faces forever. Could he make a sacrifice for the sake of family unity? He wondered if he might find true love with Malvika, and if it would mean letting go of his fantasy of being with Tara. Perhaps he and Tara were never meant to be. He felt a mix of emotions as he watched his parents - happiness for their happiness and pain at the thought of losing Tara. He closed the door, took a moment to say goodbye to Tara in his mind, and then went to his room. With tears in his eyes, he picked up his phone and texted Malvika.

"Will you be my Wilson, throughout?"

***

25th December 2016- The Wedding Day

Malvika said yes, they met sometimes, chatted a lot on phone, at times on calls. They enjoyed camaraderie of each other a lot and in no time the marriage was fixed, horoscopes were got matched by Malvika's parents and 24 gunas were matched out of total 36 which can be considered a get go for marriage. A safe zone to get married! The auspicious date, as per horoscopes, was in three months. The relationship had started building a little by little, brick by brick. It was less of a romantic but more of a caring and affectionate kind of relationship so far. And both had given time to establish this relationship slowly. And here they were, the D Day. The strong red threads between two spirits were finally formed!

Malvika became the part of Avi's family. And slowly became an important one, one without whom it was impossible for everyone to survive. Everyone had got so dependent on her that at times it felt like impossible that how on earth they were even living their lives till now. From his dad's medicines, the food, taking care of the house, managing all the rituals which as per Hindu customs and traditions are umpteen. Taking care of the young ones, their needs, tuition them for their studies, letting all the family members come together like one big family, and yes, taking care of Avi. In no time she became the centre of universe of this small family, where for any need, any requirement, the first name and may be the last as well at times, was Malvika. It was almost like everyone was under her enchanting spell. Malvika knew where each thing of the house was, from pin to plane. Everyone was not just dependent on Malvika but so affectionate for her that they just followed whatever she had to say with lot of affection. Little did everyone knew what they are getting themselves into. When she became the most prominent person of the house, no one knew. It was almost like she knew how to make everyone dance to her tunes. Everyone used to believe what she showed or expressed, her sweet words, her kid like innocence, no one knew what was in her heart including Avi.

Human psychology works in mysterious ways. Everything looks cool and good till the time your own authority, position, worth is challenged, either directly or indirectly. Funny part is, that many times it is not even there! It's all in the mind. But when it hits, it hits hard than one can perceive.

What used to be seen as sweet, affection, care, was now being seen as interference, accost, becoming a "sovereign" which otherwise his mom was till now.

"How much care she has!" had become "how much dare she has! ". And as happens with every happy family in the world, the happiness and unity started to wither and came out only in the public to show how happy, content, their family was!

You cannot keep two shillings in the same pocket, else it will start making noise. Three options, first, keep them in separate pockets, second, make provisions for both in the same pocket, third, enjoy the music!

Chivalry becomes rivalry! Sportsman spirit dooms! Fedal becomes "Fade-ALL"! Those tiniest of emotions starts erupting which no one knew. Jealousy, bringing down the other, maligning, and what not. It becomes a silent boxing match, where the sole purpose is to K.O. the other, but not with hands, with tactics. A fight of power!! A fight of who the man of the house is!

In any group, community, family, one thing remains common. When there is a fight between two, the others are judged by their choice like with whom they are standing.

Diplomacy is not everyone's cup of tea but those who can be diplomatic are the real winners. But those who are unblessed with this tactic suffer more than those who are fighting. They will always be judged for the side they take.

Avi was no different. He used to feel helpless mostly as it used to be so difficult to even understand who is right and who is not. For his mom it was like, "you will always be on your wife's side" and for Malvika, "You don't care about me" or "You don't take stands for me, don't speak up for me". Someone has put it up nicely, "Marriage is like a walk in Park, Jurassic Park!"

If every cloud has a silver lining, then sometimes the vice versa is true as well. No one can be that perfect, there is always something that goes on in deeper level. She used to be what everyone expected her to be. She was proficient enough to turn over the loopholes of Avi family in her favour, almost like divide and rule. Avi became the punching bag from both sides. He became a garbage bin. At one side his mom used to vent out everything Malvika said and Malvika used to do the same for his mom. Sometimes there used to be serious emotional draining sessions where Avi used to sit in front of them, one by one, and take all the emotions they just offloaded. Those emotions, it had so melodrama, so many cries, so many blames, so much hatred, so much hullabaloo, which started hitting Avi. Even when there were no roasting sessions like this for Avi, even then, the atmosphere back at home was so unbearable, as no one was talking to each other and sitting in distant places away from each other, it used to make his head go crazy.

Avi used to go numb sometimes and sometimes he just could not sleep the whole night thinking about all those talks or the emotions. And then, like a miracle, in no time, they both used to be together again as if nothing really happened!! And like they are the world's best mom in law and daughter in law! Then there is love flowing, out of nowhere. Hugging, kissing each other, praising each other. Fun part, even then Avi used to get criticism. "We care for you, that's why we fight. We fight for you! Since we both want your good. And you? You are so careless. Don't even think about home. Always busy with office or friends. How much we wait for you. How much we want you to be here with us and enjoy smallest of moments. You are so irresponsible Avi." It seemed there was no respite for him, from either side.

Although this mother-in-law – daughter in law saga is like very common in every household, almost like some profound karmic connect which gives lot of opportunities and lessons to grow if taken wisely. But Avi couldn't handle it well. He started to absorb all the negativity of all the chaos and drifts into his spirit. He couldn't acknowledge the fact of his own weaknesses of lack of self-love, fear of losing and too much sensitivity tied him back to take appropriate actions at right time. He was becoming that sponge where Malvika kept off loading her complaints of smallest things so did his mom and dad. The girl, once he thought has come to bind everyone, was playing a different game of manipulations altogether. Avi who was so close to his mom, started to drift away from her and from other family members too.

Avi was fully committed to supporting Malvika in every way, even if it meant going against his family. He showered her with care and affection and tried to fulfil most of her demands. Malvika also seemed to care for him, but it was all part of a business deal. For her, marriage was like owning a person, and her care and love came with many conditions. At first, Avi thought this was just how a marriage works, with each partner expecting the other to conform to their idea of the perfect partner, and expecting them to give their time, money, and space. But this was not the kind of love that Avi knew or had ever imagined. For him, love was about setting someone free, not binding them. He believed that if we bind someone in a relationship, whether it be marriage or otherwise, it is not truly love, but only a faint illusion of it. For him, true love was about being happy seeing the other person happy, putting their joy and happiness above our own needs. Such questions used to run in his mind, but he used to brush them off because he thought maybe he is crazy to think about this kind of pure real love. May be in real life Malvika version humans is what is true and Tara epitome just happen in dreams or some fantasy world. Maybe he never belonged to this strange world. He started to lose himself completely not because of just this family chik chik, but there was more to this whole experience, something darker was into play.

'Malvika I am planning a trip to Goa with my office colleagues' Avi said in polite yet firm tone.

'Oh ok, but I will be left alone, what about me?' in sweetest of voice yet in agitated tone replied Malvika.

'What do you mean, just last month we went to Shimla.' Surprised Avi said.

'Yes, I know, but I also want to go Goa, I know you will check out hot girls out there." like a kid Malvika responded.

'I want to get away for a while Malvika, can't I have even two days of my own "me" time?' Irritated Avi said in a bit high tone.

'Yes Yes, you can have Avi, but you can also have that with me. We will have lot of fun and romantic moments", winked Malvika in flirting tone, looking deep into his eyes while putting her hands around Avi. "Also, I will take care of you, like I always do. Your little things where you need me."

Avi melted, his head like swirled for a while, and replied in hazy state, "Okay sweetie, as you say."

A long smile welcomed her face and like she won some battle. She departed away to make Avi's favourite cuisine. Avi couldn't understand what happened just now. First time in his two years of marriage he asked something from Malvika, which she not only refused to give but also somehow made him agree to adhere to what she wanted. What hit him was he had strongly determined before talking to her, to make this trip happen, as he needed firmly this 'me time' for his regeneration. His head started to swirl more and suddenly he experienced a sharp pain in his heart. Something is not right Avi, at all deep down, his heart said very loudly this time and he listened and agreed that indeed, something was not right!

We often ignore the warning our soul give to us, which lead to more drastic consequences. This Tom and Jerry game became part of their lives. His health was taking a toll. He had started spending more time in the office to avoid the melodrama or the atmosphere or energies, back home. He started going to after office parties which he used to avoid till now. His intake of alcohol increased due to all this and smokes too. When a person takes stress, he tries to find an easy way to get hold of it or to at least be away from it for some time. Then come these addictions! Addictions are nothing but what your mind tries to like to give you a quick relief. A quick solution. A shortcut! We feel that these addictions are helping us but in fact they don't. They just supress the emotion or deflect it, for some time. But they don't solve anything. On the contrary they act as a *catalyst* as we don't solve the issue heads on but supress or deflect. It is like something has been put to a hidden folder which still consumes the ROM but we are happy as we are not seeing it, at least. Plus, the ill effects it brings on our health otherwise, also doesn't make any good to us. His hairs started turning grey, prematurely. His belly started showing a geometric progression in inches. Other ailments related to lungs, heart started to surface a little, but not very prominent to be seen in clinical tests. But he could see it! Everyone knows his or her body the best. We know, a lot of times, what's happening inside us and the causative factors. But we keep wearing masks on our face as if nothing's happening. Our mind again starts playing like, oh it is okay. This happens! Oh, you are ageing. Ageing brings these issues. See almost everyone in your circle has it or is near to it or at least started.

We keep ignoring. Amidst all these things, the worst part was, no one in his home could even feel this change in him or rather, the real reasons of it!

Time was flying. It had been three years since Avi and Malvika got married. Insecurities and chaos were increasing more and more. His health was deteriorating a lot inside. His belly had become bulgy. His addictions were increasing. He was consuming more alcohol and smokes now, which his family did not know. They were under pure impression that he consumes it within limits as with time, a person becomes master in hiding how much he has consumed these addictions. He had become a good actor. He used to come home late. He had become "Manjulika" in its own way. He peculiarly knew when his family will be slept and are into REM Sleep, everyone. He used to come home only by then. Malvika used to sleep like a baby. She was blessed with good sleep. So, Avi used to call her late in the night, after party, reaching home to open the door. She would come to open the door in her, this, sleepy mode on, and would go back to bed in fraction of seconds with snores again. This way, Avi was not getting caught ever! His plan was working! This plan was worth or not nobody knew.

He was living in a two-dimensional world. At one, he was a good actor, showing everyone how happy he is and used to laugh a lot with his colleagues. He was the centre of attraction of any party or meeting. Everyone used to be like how chirpy he is. How happy he is! No one knew how lonely and depressed he was inside.

Human Psychology! A person who laughs a lot, tries to be centre of attraction always, is deep lonely and sad inside. The worst part, at that point of time, a person is not able to tell this all to his people. No one needs Mercy but love. We fear of telling the naked truth to others as we don't ourselves want to see it. If ever, once in blue moon, Avi tried to take stand for his own self too, Malvika used to gaze at him with piercing eyes or mumble something in her mouth, which like instantly prevented him to take even one step further in that direction.

One day, there was a huge cat fight back at home. When Avi reached home, the things had already taken a bizarre turn. There was all negative energy in the home. His mom was reading something at farthest corner possible of his home, with an angry face, with all the lines of forehead, from Saturn line to ground line, making a perfect symmetrical statistical bell curve. Something big had happened, Avi reckoned. Indeed, something big had happened. His mom and mom in law had an exchange of some words and Malvika was frowning as how his mom can talk bad about and to her mom and his mom was angry like his mom in law don't deserve any respect as her daughter doesn't respect us, among several things. The situation was so horrid, that it had cries, silence, distance, anger, victimisation, hatred, judgements, opinions, and any negative emotional word one can imagine.

"Please take me to my mom's place. May be no one wants me to be here. May be no one loves me here. I am not good enough. May be your family had dreamt of a better girl than me. I should leave probably, forever. There is not one good reason to stay here when there is no love and respect for me. And when my own husband is silently listening to everything and not taking stands for me or can fight for my respect, its better I go for the betterment of everyone. May be after I leave everyone will be happy, including you." Malvika said it all sobbing.

Avi had tears in his eyes too. He had listened a lot of things from Malvika in the past, but today it was way emotional for him to handle. He went to his mom, agitated, and tried to talk to him. Like a typical Punjabi mom, she played a reverse Uno with her tears and cries and like how Avi has become a puppet of Malvika. He doesn't want to even understand his mom's take. All he wants is to show how good Malvika is as if she is bad etc. etc.

Avi had a bad migraine, as usual, after this fight. He used to have a lot of migraines with normal to severe headaches as well. He was famous in his office for having a packet of aspirin tablets in his drawer. In case anyone used to feel headache in his office, they knew, Avi will have aspirin for sure. Avi used to consume it like once in three days, normally, at times to soothe the after-party hangover in the morning and also the migraines he used to get out of home negativities. This day as well, he had bad migraine after this convo with Malvika first and then his mom. Everyone had dinner silently, and then went to sleep. After all the big screen melodrama what happened this night, everyone slept in like no time. Avi was awake as usual. He was emotionally lost and was down like anything. These three years had been emotionally draining for him where he was drowning. He used to have sleepless nights, crying nights, listening to sad songs and ghazals at times and feeling how lonely he is. How loveless his life had become, where there was everyone loving him for their own emptiness and not just to give love. Selfish love everywhere he used to feel and the motives and emotions of everyone. He was broken or rather shattered. He stood up and went to the small temple in his house. He saw each god's statue with tearful eyes and started conversing with them.

"Are you for real? No! You can't be! All of you are mere statues and nothing. There is no one up there, I totally know it now. Or even if you are there, then you have forgot that there is a man in this world whose name is Avi. Don't you feel any compassion for me? Don't you feel any mercy on me? What have I done to live this kind of life? Why? Just tell me why? You want me to light incense sticks and lamps for you like four times a day? Will you be happy if I recite Arti's and prayers daily? Just tell me what you want??"

He saw Shiva's statue and his eyes froze. He so loved Shiva since he was a child.

"Why Shiva? How can you let this all happen to me without any pause even to take a breath? You have been so important part of my life since always, even when I don't offer the daily prayers, you have been there inside my heart always. How can you be so indifferent to my pains? You have given even asura's, boons. But you cannot even take these pains away from my life? What kind of a GOD are you? Or have you lost your powers? Or you don't want to help me? Or do you need any bribe? What???" Avi had gone crazy due to this emotional pain he was feeling.

"I don't want to follow you all anymore. I am a disbeliever in you now onwards, an atheist! Coz no GOD can give someone so pains when that person has done no wrong in his life. I have not even crushed an ant with my legs, intentionally. Have never given any pain, physical or emotional, to any one with my actions. Have never demanded anything from my parents or you people. Have always given love to even those who did bad to me. I keep on forgetting all the bad anyone has done to me and give them all the compassion again and again. I keep on forgetting bad things and forgiving people for those deeds, not for any favour but since I can't just think bad of anyone. And what do I get in return like always? This? Why this love remains unrequited. Am I not a human being? What am I, who am I? Just go away you all. You all don't matter to me anymore. If I am non-existent to you, then you all too are non-existent to me. Good Riddance!!!"

With this, he came back to his room with all the tears in his eyes. His tears must have filled two buckets full if those teardrops would have been collected. He lied on his side of the bed, and as usual, started staring the ceiling, with tears falling from his eyes trickling down through his side boards then ears then neck and then finally settling down at his pillow.

He had contemplated ending his life before, but this time the desire was stronger than ever. He had made a firm promise to himself that he no longer wished to live! His mind was consumed with dark and overwhelming suicidal thoughts. He felt trapped in a labyrinth of life, where even the notion of true love seemed out of reach. Compassion and understanding seemed to elude him, even from those closest to him.

He had tried to find the strength to take control of his life, but something always seemed to hold him back. He couldn't shake the feeling that his wife, Malvika, was somehow responsible for this suffocating sense of stagnation. Even in their most intimate moments, he felt nothing in his body or heart. He, who had once been a true romantic at heart, was now numb to the idea of love. He knew he was trapped, but his willpower had become so weak that he couldn't even take a single step towards freedom. He was amid a "dark night of the soul" with not a glimmer of light in sight. He tried to even talk to his mom and dad about it. How he is no happier and feel suffocated in this marriage. His health is going down. But as expected all he used to get was, 'All this happens in marriage, you will have to suffice', 'think about society', 'we all had lots of fights and here we are still together. For whom? You!' etc etc. They were not even willing to listen to even his single plea. They couldn't understand it was not even about fights anymore, it was matter of his survival now. And he was not talking about the usual fights, or usual things happen between husband and wife. It was something strange, something else, something even he could not recognise or comprehend fully. He was short of words to put it the way he felt inside in front of his parents. Since no one understand and consider depression as a real thing, but it's as life threatening as cancer can be, if not treated at time.

Avi had no more will to live now. The circumstances in his life made him feel like an ultimate victim. His mind then started to making plans. "Will take a term plan insurance soon for as much cover as is possible with my income. After earning for some 5-6 or 10 years, enough for Malvika to lead a good life with my savings and investments, her own salary, and with the proceeds of this insurance cover I will have, I will end my life!"

"This remaining life, I will live like a lifeless human. A numb human. Happiness is not meant for me so will not even think about it. Will work hard to get as much earning as I can throughout this period which Malvika will get after me. This is how it is gonna be now. This is my life now!"

As the dust settled and life resumed its familiar rhythms, Avi's household returned to its customary cheer. His mother and wife laughed and chatted as if nothing had ever happened. But for Avi, everything had changed! He had fully embraced atheism and was now determined to live by a new mantra: "Work until 45, then disappear!"

He began to meticulously document his investments, savings, and liabilities, as well as all his assets, in a journal, which he planned to give to his wife just before he vanished from the face of the earth. He would tell her it was important for her to know these things, without revealing his true intentions.

In the meantime, Avi withdrew into himself, speaking and smiling only when it was necessary to avoid causing any more scenes in the household. But even then, his words and actions were nothing more than a facade.

His split personality was zooming like never. The same was with his colleagues and friends. He used to be silent mostly, but when he used to sense that after a while someone may ask him questions like is he okay or something like that, he used to crack a joke or start talking to people with smile and laughter. Weird it was, but then there seemed no other option to his mind than this. He still was involved in his after-office parties as it was much better than to be at home. At least, he had a positive company. There was laughter, joy around in the parties. This way, he was living a robotic life.

He had become big time insomniac. In the night he mostly used to either see ceiling all the time, lying numb, or used to listen to some music, sad music!

Months passed by; he was working as per the plan. Work till 45 and leave. He had no motive no intent, nothing, to survive. Nothing used to entice him. He had no taste for food any long. He just used to eat food to be living. He had no choices in anything. Moribund his life had become. On one of those nights, one day, he got a message on his cell phone, when he was lying like a dead man on the bed, watching the ceiling.

"Hi. Is this Avi?" A message from an unknown number appeared.

Avi kept his phone to the side table again. He was not at all interested in who it was. A message beeped again after a while.

"Mauri!" A message from the same unknown number appeared.

Avi saw it and again put it down on his side table without giving it any thought. He was numb, zoned out, as ever. After a few moments, as if sudden realisation appeared, he took his phone again in his hand and saw the messages again. "Mauri!" He saw this word again and again as if could not believe what he was looking at.

He immediately replied, "Gauri!! Is it you?"

"Glad you could recognise, Mana :)", a message came from the other side.

"Of course! How can I forget my dear Mauri! Haha. How are you? How have you been and where were you from past so many years. I guess we are connecting almost like how much, 14-16 years!? My goodness. Time flies! How did you get my number?" Avi bombarded Gauri with lot of questions out of excitement.

"Got your number from a social media profile of yours. I will talk to you Avi in some days as am going for an assignment and about to board a flight for US. The number will also be off for a week or so till am there plus would be occupied quite a lot but will connect to you as and when I reach back. It really gives me immense pleasure to talk to you again Avi. Take care!" Gauri texted.

"Sure Gauri. Have a safe flight and stay in the US. Strange it is that you somehow found my number on my profile and here we are chatting after so many years." Avi responded.

Avi, Gauri and Tanmay were the closest of friends, bonded together through their shared experiences in school. They spent all their time together, studying, playing, and exploring. They were the best of buddies. One day, while studying about Maori culture for a school assignment, they came across three words that resonated with them deeply - "Mauri," "Mana," and "Tapu." These words spoke to the interconnectedness of people and nature, and Gauri, with her interest in spirituality and yoga, found parallels with these words in the texts she studied. To her, "Mana" was like "Prana," the vital energy that flows through all things. Mauri as 'Consciousness or chitta" and "Tapu" was like an essence or parameter of growth, and it could be seen as it reflected in the aura of both living and non-living. Since Tanmay was quite handsome, strong build, bright, and had a spark in him he was given the nickname "Tapu". Avi being very energetic and very sensitive too in emotions, was given the name "Mana". And Gauri, since she was the one who used to bind this small group together and since her name sounded similar, became "Mauri". She used to say, "Both Chitta and Prana interact with each other for life to exist.

Everything in this world is a combination of Purusha and Prakriti, or in a way, Mauri and Mana." Avi and Tanmay used to laugh a lot on her these spiritual talks back then, but they loved these names though. It was fun to call each other by names other than their real ones. It was like a thrilling game for both, which gave them a kind of adrenaline rush. It was like "their thing". And ever since they adopted these names, they used to call each other by these names only. Time flew by, and after 10th standard, their choice of subjects was different. While Tanmay chose fine arts and went abroad for studying, Gauri chose science and moved to some other school. Avi chose commerce and stayed back in the same school.

As the years passed, the bonds of the trio slowly frayed. Though they stayed in touch for a while, they eventually got caught up in their own lives. In those days, communication wasn't as easy as it is now. Cell phones were a luxury only the wealthy could afford, and the cost of even an incoming call was exorbitant. Pagers were the closest thing to a mobile device, but they could only send short text messages and were even rarer than cell phones. He couldn't help but recall how Tanmay's dad used to boast about his Motorola pager, always keeping it prominently displayed on his waistband.

Avi was lost in all these memories and after a good period, had a smile on his face. He had like almost forgotten about Gauri and Tanmay since it had been so many years. He closed his eyes and tried to fall asleep when his phone gave a text beep again. It was Gauri!

"Hey. The network had lost while I was boarding. I searched for you Avi on the internet and that is how I landed on your social page and got your number. I have been getting dreams and visions about you that you are not well. I saw you drowning, not once but like at least a dozen times. I saw you falling into some lake which is filled with hot burning Lava. It seemed as if you are losing it. I tried holding your hands, but you seemed not interested to save your own self due to your emotional downstate. I tried so much to hold your hands, but you were withering. I had these dreams a lot of times and, also while meditating I am getting similar visions of you being not happy in your life and as if you don't want to live anymore! Am going through an awakening for some time and can see visions and dreams, very vividly. Okay, Avi! The crew is asking to switch off the phones now. Bye. Will soon contact you. And listen! Don't worry. Things will be fine, whatever it is. Everyone sees the night but, the morning too. The sun will rise, Avi! The turbulence will end, just keep holding on to something, anything. Take Care!"

Avi was dumbstruck. How Gauri got to know about his present state? Dreams, visions, is this for real? What does it mean? Avi could not sleep the whole night but for a different reason that day.

Chapter 6

Gauri

When everything seems to fail,

When there is nothing to avail,

When you cry out loud for someone,

Some angel will, somehow, find its summon!

Gauri's words were still banging in Avi's head. Dreams about him and Visions, He was really surprised about these things. "How can she know my current state when we have not talked to each other for years? And she said she is going through some awakening. What was that?" Avi was perplexed to the core.

Avi had seen a transfer this year, and it had been a few months since he had shifted to Udaipur. Udaipur is a beautiful city in the Aravali Mountain range of Rajasthan. Aravali is believed to be one of the oldest mountain ranges in India, some belief it to be even older than the Himalayas. And because of its wear and tear from so many years and changes in geographical conditions across the world, these mountains have depreciated like anything and are now a dwarf mountain range but a long one, which ranges from Rajasthan to Madhya Pradesh. Udaipur is also called "Venice of the east", the city of lakes. It is home to some very famous lakes like Fatehsagar, Lake Pichhola, Swaroop

Sagar, Jaisamand Lake etc. Interestingly, some lakes are so beautifully surrounding the city, also within it, that they are connected to each other. The city is also known for its abundance of zinc and marble.

Udaipur is a city renowned for its rich cultural heritage, boasting a variety of historical forts, palaces, museums, galleries, and a unique Solar Observatory located on Fateh Sagar Lake. Visitors can also enjoy the city's picturesque gardens, architectural temples and sites, and traditional fairs such as the "Shilpgram Utsav," which typically takes place over 10 days. Historically, Udaipur was the capital of the Mewar kingdom and is in southern Rajasthan, near the border of Gujarat. The city is also a popular location for destination weddings and film shoots. Despite its romantic atmosphere, Avi felt distant from experiencing true love in this enchanting city.

Every day he used to think about what Gauri had said, trying to decipher its meaning. "Gauri" as this name echoed in his mind and heart, suddenly like he was transferred to another era of his life. Almost like a breath of fresh cool breeze touched his soul. He always had this niche, she was not an ordinary girl, and there had always been something special about her. Just like that he floated away into his past when he first met her. Gauri was a simple girl in childhood. She had a keen interest in religion, mythology, Spirituality and Yoga since always. She used to read a lot of books on these occult topics whereas Avi and Tanmay used to be busy with their video games or other outside sports like cricket, Tennis and Swimming. Gauri always used to be engrossed in reading. She used to take part in elocution contests in the school, especially on these topics and with her wisdom she always used to stand out in the crowd. However, since Avi and Tanmay knew nothing about these topics, it used to bore them a little. They used to make fun of her and used to pull her out of the library sometimes. But still, Avi always used to be in awe of Gauri, her mysterious yet warm vibe always used to make him a question, who on earth is she?

Despite Gauri's reluctance to join in on the fun, Avi and Tanmay always tried to include her in their school adventures. The three of them formed a perfect balance as friends. Avi was the one who first convinced Gauri to skip class when he wanted to buy guavas from a local vendor behind the school. One day, Avi and Tanmay made a secret plan to take Gauri with them after recess. They removed some temporary stones from the boundary wall of the school, creating a space for them to cross over to the other side. They then forcibly dragged Gauri with them, despite her protests and attempts to run back to class. Gauri was terrified, thinking she would be expelled, but Avi and Tanmay were laughing and enjoying themselves. They ate the guavas and spent some time wandering around the streets, while Gauri repeatedly begged to go back to school.

"Tanmay and Avi, let's go back!" said Gauri with anxiety.

Suddenly Tanmay's face changed expressions as if he saw some ghost.

"What happened Tanmay?" Asked Gauri worriedly.

"Nothing, it felt like I saw something, some light or what, don't know. Ouch!! My head, as if someone putting pressure" Tanmay said it all with discomfort inside.

Avi teased him, "You and your weird experiences, are you high on something or what?'

But Gauri knew Tanmay felt some unseen force, perhaps a wandering spirit, she always believed that what these naked eyes can't see doesn't mean it's not true. 'If you want to find secrets of the universe, think in terms of frequency, energy, and vibrations' words of wisdom by Nikola Tesla she always used to quote.

"It's okay Tanmay. Just take a deep breath, relax, and feel it is all part of this universe" She knew his senses are very developed.

Tanmay felt better after he did what Gauri said along with some deep breathing. He was feeling little sensations on his forehead, but he was all good otherwise.

"Come now let's go, we are getting late," Gauri said to both after knowing that Tanmay was all good as before.

"Just a little much more Gauri. It is fun, isn't it? chuckled Tanmay along with Avi.

"Oh, God! You guys, but you know what I will miss these moments" said Gauri, out of nowhere with moist eyes.

Both Avi and Tanmay were a bit taken aback but felt the same emotions almost like it travelled to their hearts. Silently the trio, went back to their classroom, before the start of a new class, and luckily survived the bunk where the teacher did not notice missing three kids in the class of 60. Their fun activities used to be a refreshing change for her to bring back from her realm of unknown and unseen to reality.

Avi was overwhelmed with a flood of memories as if they were playing out like a movie in his mind. He had always held Gauri in high esteem, admiring her intelligence, wisdom, and knowledge. Even though he often teased her, he had a deep respect for her. He used to gift her books that he thought she would enjoy, and she often liked the books he picked out. They had a special bond where Avi knew Gauri's likes and dislikes well and Gauri could sense what Avi was feeling, what he wanted and what he was going through. She took care of him like a motherly figure, understanding his sensitive side and how he felt neglected as a child in his home. She knew how hard he tried to hide his pain behind his laughter, and she could sense the unspoken.

Though she always had a tough time, as he was a naughty kid. But deep inside in his heart, Avi knew, she had a very important role to play in his journey of life, though in such an age we brush off such insights. So did Gauri, she knew this connection with Avi is much more than a normal school friendship. He was a gifted soul with a much bigger purpose, just it was not the time yet to reveal it, perhaps.

She used to take him to the library to read books. She was like, read any book, whatever you like, but read. It will expand your horizon and your consciousness. You can derive knowledge from any book. You never know what kind of jewel you may find in any book.

"You know about Panchatantra, right? It is a fiction basically but has a deep meaning to be learnt. We can derive knowledge, wisdom, and lessons from any book. If it is hard for you to read a heavy book on self-development or spirituality, you can read fiction or anything you may like. But read! It will help you manifold." Gauri always used to say this to Avi.

Avi liked her company more than those books. So, while she used to dive deep into her kind of books, he would find an easy book to read on and at times comics. But one thing he always used to make sure of was to take care of Gauri while she is reading. To fetch her water to drink, food, snacks, juices etc., most of the time without even she asking for it. He used to shhh everyone in the library while she is focused on something. Their bond was beautiful. He loved to see her reading with such concentration.

While Avi and Gauri were in the library reading one day, Avi suddenly looked at Gauri and felt as if time had stopped. In that moment, he saw Gauri as a goddess or angel, surrounded by a bright light and with wings coming out of her back. He felt a strange sense of devotion towards her and an intense urge to touch her feet for blessings. In a trance-like state, he reached out and touched her feet. Gauri quickly pulled away and shouted, "Avi! What are you doing?" Avi was left confused and couldn't understand what had just happened. Gauri took him out of the library while he was still in a state of bewilderment.

"What happened to you? Why were you touching my feet like that?" Gauri asked surprised.

"I don't know. I got a huge respect for you that moment and out of it touched your feet. It was like am touching the feet of some goddess or some guru of mine. It was bizarre I know, but I just could not help it" Avi responded with utter shock and amusement.

"Oh! It might be related to our previous births or higher realms. You might have also crossed different timelines at that moment. It is like a déjà vu moment where you interacted with some other birth of yours, where I was also there and probably in that birth or realm, I am your guru or something. It can be from some other galaxy or time zone as well which crossed, in a way, because of your strong will or something else. It can also be something from the future of this life or it can be something from our soul or spirit world, which just crossed your way. Don't know.'

"Excuse me?"

"Hmmm! May be some other day." Gauri said it with a smile and discussion ended.

Avi will always remember the day he last saw Gauri and Tanmay, their farewell day. Gauri wore a beautiful lavender saree while Tanmay and Avi dressed in tuxedos. Tanmay couldn't take his eyes off her, revealing to Avi that he had a secret crush on her. Avi knew that there was something more than just friendship in Tanmay's heart. He couldn't help but tease Tanmay, "C'mon now, you have to tell me Tanmay, this secret you are hiding."

"Ummm what?" Tanmay asked, startled.

"How do you feel about Gauri?" Avi asked seriously.

"She's nice," Tanmay stammered nervously.

"Hahaha, you can't fool me," Avi snickered.

"Do you think she likes me?" Tanmay asked anxiously.

"That only she can tell. Why don't you ask her out?" Avi insisted.

"I'm afraid, man. What if she takes it the wrong way? I don't want to spoil our friendship," Tanmay replied.

"Hmm, it's a tough choice, but if not now, then when?" Avi said.

"Maybe someday. Who knows what the future holds for us," Tanmay said, looking sad.

Gauri, who had just walked up to them, smiled, and said, "We'll meet again." She heard their last line and tried to lighten the mood by suggesting "Remember that song what Alan sings in 'Hangover?'"

"And we're the three best friends that anybody could have, We're the three best friends that anyone could have, We're the three best friends that anyone could have, and we'll never, never, ever, ever, ever leave each other!!", They

laughed incessantly while rhyming to it for so many times holding each other's hand in ring-a-ring o' roses.

"Come, let's have a group hug" Gauri said with wet eyes, and they hugged, with tears in their eyes, almost having a feeling like parting with their own family, which in such short course of time, became so much closely bonded than their own family.

"I have a strong feel one day we three will meet again", Avi Said.

The time has come, said Avi to himself as he came back to present moment checking his phone once again.

Seven days passed, with Avi thinking about Gauri and Tanmay, but mostly about Gauri. He anxiously waited for Gauri to call him, wanting to know and understand more about her. However, Gauri did not call, even after ten days had passed. Avi tried her number multiple times out of curiosity and anxiety, but it was always switched off. On the eleventh day, he finally received a call from Gauri.

"Avi! How are you? My stay in the US got extended a few days due to an unfinished project I was working on, so I couldn't call you."

"I'm good, Gauri. Yeah, I waited a lot for your call, and even tried your number but it was always switched off. Didn't you have any other number while you were in the US?"

"I had a temporary international number, Avi, but I didn't want to talk to you on it," she replied.

"Why not?" he asked.

"These numbers aren't safe for calling or even texting, especially international numbers," she said, sounding cautious.

"Oh, yeah. Phones are getting tapped these days," Avi said.

"No, it's not just tapping. Conversations can even be traced by darker forces who want to gain an edge over light by tracking down information," Gauri explained.

"Sorry, I didn't understand that" Avi said, confused.

"I know. Don't worry, things will be clearer in some time. How have you been?" Gauri changed the topic.

They chatted for about an hour. Avi told her about his life, a little bit of it, not complete. They talked about their childhood memories, laughed a lot remembering those days, and about their current lives, professional lives.

"So, what do you do, professionally. What this project was for which you had went to US?"

"Iam a Principal Investigator in Archaeology with one of the leading Indian firms."

"Wow! That is impressive. I had been happier and shouting out of the full strength of my lungs, if I could understand even an iota about this designation and career of yours, huh!"

"Haha! You and your bad jokes. It did not change with time, huh?"

"Getting better day by day! Winks!"

"Yeah Yeah! Okay, so my job consists of conducting and supervising all the aspects of archaeological projects and studies. This includes archaeological, cultural, geological, historical, and environmental research; Preparing and maintaining records; archaeological investigations and due diligence surveys. Archaeological resource identification and assessment; treatment plans, data recovery, and mitigation; archaeological, cultural, and historical artefact and laboratory analysis; preparation of a variety of archaeological documentation and technical reports; and preparing artefacts and records for curation."

"But you were always so interested in spirituality and mythology, how is this connected to that and is it even helping you?" Asked confused Avi.

"Well, you see, archaeology is the key to finding so many hidden secrets about our mythology. I am getting to know so much about our ancient temples, related stories, and proofs with so many artefacts. Do you know what's the beauty of this? I can actually connect this knowledge with spirituality. For eg, why temples, and pyramids are all triangle in shape from above? Because triangles are concentrator portals which when aligned right, channel immense divine energy and amplify the concentration during meditation or devotion dhyana. Also, our heart or Anhata chakra shape has two infused triangles making it a star. One star is pointing upwards while the other is pointing down. We also know it as the 'Star of David'.

Avi was spellbound.

"While some projects are within the domestic bounds, some take me to far-flung areas, at times posh like US and at times, even the remotest villages of Africa where there is no sign of even electricity, forget about mobile networks, but it's like a treasure of hidden mysteries and ancient long-lost secrets." She told with enthusiasm.

"Oh! So, you people found mummies and dinosaurs!" chuckled Avi.

"One of us. Anyways. We must talk about much more important than this!" she suddenly sounded serious.

"I am all ears" he was curious.

"Well, Avi, as I had mentioned to you in the last call, I am going through an awakening, a spiritual awakening, where I am able to see, manifest, a lot of things much clearly than ever, even those things which are unseen. I have been into profound spiritual practices for some time where my *Chakras* have opened quite a lot and have received a lot of spiritual gifts.' She tried to explain to him.

"Yes, I remember even in school days you were always engrossed in spiritual books, trying to understand and solve God knows what mysteries" teased Avi.

'Hahah, yeah Avi, so you remember".

"Well, hard to forget a crazy girl" he teased.

Laughed Gauri and continued further, "With these gifts and practices, I have been connecting with the divine, getting guidance in shape of visions, dreams etc. I have also seen a lot of my previous births, including some with you as well, and have learnt why a lot of things happening the way it is. About the relationships like how most of our relations in family are karmic, and not at soul level so that we can learn our lessons to evolve further. Mostly lessons are about overcoming our weaknesses which are fuelled by attachments and desires. We are mostly blinded by this idea of love in the name of which we keep getting hurt and hurt others. It's mostly our insecurities and not even iota of pure love. This binds us in this never-ending cycle of birth and death".

Avi finally understood what Gauri meant, as if somewhere deep inside, he already knew it. It was as if someone had come along and reminded him of it, like dust being brushed off to reveal a shiny surface.

"I have become an atheist, Gauri. One night I even shouted at Shiva, who I always felt a connection with. Remember? I blamed him for not helping me and for putting me in this never-ending maze of sorrows," Avi said, tears streaming down his face. "What have I done to deserve this, Gauri? I am so tired now." He was completely broken.

Gauri took a deep breath and spoke in a calm and compassionate voice. "Your mind is making you play the victim, Avi. You are resisting what is happening. Remember, no one forced you into these circumstances. It's a choice your spirit made before coming to this world. There is a reason behind it, deeper lessons and understanding. But because of these blocks, we are not able to see it and we tie ourselves to this never-ending pattern of sorrow and despair. Shiva, Shakti, or Shyam, they are not just someone outside of us, they are a part of our consciousness inside us. Shakti represents 'The Prana', our conscious mind, senses, energy, and body, or Prakriti. While Shiva represents or manifests 'The Yog', our subconscious, 'the spirit' inside us, the Purusha. And Shyam represents our 'Soul', oneness in love, Bhakti, or flow. The spiritual journey begins from the body to the soul."

Avi listened to it all in silence and with utmost concentration. A lot of things reminded him immediately of Tara, and she used some of these words like chakras, pure love, and all too. A sudden lump formed in his throat as he remembered Tara.

"I have been meditating a lot lately, reading good books, and learning a lot about spirituality. I used to meditate even before, but the way it is now, it's something else. I am trying to control my mind, senses, and overcome my weaknesses and karmas. It's a bit time-consuming process. Sometimes, in deep meditation states, my spirit also travels and floats astrally, but I am well aware and conscious at that time."

"During such states, the visions I get at times, and in my dreams while I am asleep, I have seen you drowning into a well or pool of fire. I saw a huge white room, where you are slowly walking towards this giant pool of fire. I am like outside on ceiling of terrace and through a window I called your name, gave my hand, but you like a zombie paid no heed. Perhaps, like you are under some deep spell and under loads of your own emotions. Come what may I tried always; you didn't pay heed, I have woken up a lot of times panting after seeing that, with my face full of sweat and my body drained. It has started to increase off late where I am seeing you like in every other dream or vision. I tried to come to you astrally as well, but you have blocked yourself a lot due to these weights you are carrying on your shoulders and I just could not touch your soul. That is when I decided to search for you and contact you directly."

"I knew something is not right with you. I don't know Avi, how much of what I said makes sense to you presently, but I am just trying to give you some hints. And there is always a cosmic plan which is way bigger than anything we reckon. Me seeing your visions and dreams, and contacting you like this out of the blue after so many years, there must be something. The only thing that matters is, are you ready to understand all this and are up for the help the cosmos wants to give you." She tried her best to explain him.

"I understand Gauri. There was a person in my life some years back who also used to say some similar things like what you said. Chakras, kundalini etc. So, I have heard about these but don't know much about it. I was told about Third Eye Chakra a little, but it is all in my vague memories. I know Gauri that I need help but don't know what to do. Things are just going out of place for me and there seems no sunshine. You are right, am falling deep into like dark pit.

Life has become so challenging that even a single day seems like a year. Fighting a lot of battles like daily but still no hopes of getting out, ever." He sounded like a lost warrior.

"I understand Avi. But understand, that you are so drowned in the pit that there is no other option but to rise again or to stay there forever. Acknowledge this hand Avi, what I am or other people or angels or the divine are offering you. See, we all are just mediums who can help you, but it is "You" who must work on self. We can only guide you and nothing else. It's like if you are hungry, some other person can arrange food for you. But at the end, it is you who has to finally have to eat it. But if you don't have the courage or strength to eat it, even if there lies your favourite dish on the table, you won't be able to savour it! And sorry, but you said that you are fighting a lot of battles. No Avi, you are not! The battles have not even started yet for you! It is your mind which is victimising you, sympathising you that oh how much vulnerable you are, and you can do nothing. On the contrary, it is you who can change things for you and make work for you" she tried to ignite little bit of hope in him.

Suddenly Avi remembered that dream he got before he made choice to marry Malvika. The two roads dream. He told about that to Gauri. In case it is related to whatever visions she is getting.

Gauri took a deep breath, tried to see about it and said "See Avi, right now all I can say is, attachments, fear and desires is how we give powers to others. And some people make very ill use of it, they start feeding on it. You craved and desired for love because of your past and that made you blind enough to choose the darker road without even thinking of the consequences as you didn't decode the dream rightly. We always get the hints if only we can understand and see at right time", Gauri left Avi stunned with this response.

"Though I will have to look deeper about the dream and your life choices and circumstances to get the complete picture. There are lots of blocks inside you Avi, emotional, and mental, which are somehow responsible for your present state. Some are root cause, and some are just on the surface. While surface ones are easy to remove, it takes toll and time to remove the deeply rooted embedded blocks. The question is, again, are you up for it? Ready to take that first step? That first flight!' Gauri said it all bluntly maintaining a single voice tone.

Avi was listening to it all trying hard to process it. It was like a reality check for him. He was stunned to the core. Someone had stirred him up so bluntly. He didn't know what to say. He needed time to digest and process all this and Gauri was able to sense it all.

"Take your time Avi, at the end it is your choice to make my boy" making the conversation lighter.

"How you know so much of things, Gauri?"

"I have been reading a lot of books, have been meditating, getting divine guidance, and meeting a lot of people, online and offline with whom I have been discussing on these topics and also the phase am going through. One of those people, even you know."

"Who?"

"Tanmay!"

"You mean our Tanmay??"

"Yes! You remember him?" Gauri asked.

"Yesss! Of course, Gauri! How can I forget him! Huge strong fatsy, Tanmay. My partner in crime." Avi said it with all the excitement of world.

'He has been part of my spiritual journey, we have been helping and supporting each other since few months.' replied Gauri.

"Oh wow," said a surprised Avi. "Never thought he could be so good in spirituality and all. But yeah, he had something in him since our school days. You remember how he used to see people and talk about the colours reflecting around, and also scare us with seeing ghosts and spirits?" Avi beamed with a nostalgic vibe.

"Yes, how can I forget that", said equally nostalgic Gauri.

"I used to be most keen on expanding my horizon by gaining knowledge from our mythological and spiritual books, Vedas, yogic texts, and sutras. Tanmay out of nowhere used to just feel these unseen and unknown spiritual dimensions. Perhaps, he has been a gifted kid with his third eye (Ajna chakra) opened since his childhood." explained Gauri.

"But how come?" Asked surprised Avi.

"Well, this is not the only human birth we exercise, but had been many more in our past lives. If we bring the ultimate consciousness in any birth and realize our ultimate purpose, moving into the direction of yog (meditation) and bhakti (devotion), it all gets accumulated in our soul consciousness. If due to by some circumstances it's left incomplete, in next birth, we start exactly from there. In some cases, the yogis develop siddhis (gifts) and it get transferred to next birth. Tanmay is such case" Gauri explained.

"Oh! So, he has been a yogi in some of his past life?" Avi asked surprisingly.

"Yes Avi, and I feel so have been you someone like that. There is a reason we all met, nothing in this universe happens randomly" she looked into his eyes, on the video call, and said calmly having a wide beautiful smile.

In that moment like something stirred inside Avi, a vibration in his heart, like something inside him pushed hard.

"I want to know more Gauri, suddenly I feel like I want to go deep in this. Who am I? Why am I on earth? What am I wandering for? Why my life had been the way it has been? how can I come out of this drowning? Like how you saw my state without me telling a single soul on this earth. What is this dimension that is beyond the perception of our naked eyes but doesn't make it any less true. Help me Gauri" Avi almost pleaded.

"Woah Woah, what an excited and curious Aura you are radiating. You know the moment we question 'WHO AM I', our spiritual journey begins. I will help you Avi" Smiled an equally excited Gauri.

Chapter 7

The Foundation

When things or people lead you to thwart,

When you are no longer able to pull your cart,

Remember, there is no other Art,

Take a deep breath and make a new start!

Gauri had called Avi to meet her and Tanmay at Goa, where Gauri was living. Tanmay was based out at London now a days and was working there. He had an ancestral property at Rishikesh and was in India on holidays. There is always a cosmic plan!

It was decided to have a rendezvous at Gauri's house. It was weekend, so convenient for all of them. Gauri anyways was now working post site works of an old shiva temple project and was having a desk job presently to make reports and all, which she was managing from home itself.

There was no non-stop flight from both Udaipur and Rishikesh to Goa, so Avi and Tanmay decided to meet at Mumbai Airport where their flight was to land with a difference of just one hour and then would take the flight to goa together.

They went to a restaurant in the airport to have tea and snacks. Tanmay had changed a lot, not just physically but also nature wise. He had become much more calm and quite focused on things. In childhood, Tanmay used to speak a lot, blabber all the time. He had become quite with an evergreen smile on his face which did not change since the time they first met at airport till now when they were having refreshments. He was silent, speaking only, when necessary, otherwise just wearing that smile and looking deep into Avi's eyes. This gaze made Avi, both uncomfortable and admiring his growth as well.

"So, what are you upto Tanmay now a days. Good to see you after so many years. It's been such a long time since we guys met. I really have a remorseful kind of a feeling right now that why we did not plan to meet before. We should have, isn't it? And it seems you have grown a lot with age. This maturity I can see on your face. You seem more matured than your age." Avi broke the silence while eating the snacks.

"Well, it had been a roller coaster journey, was not easy but I guess worth it. Though I am glad you are feeling positive change in me. We are meeting as it is supposed to happen," Said Tanmay calmly.

"True! And what do you do for living?"

"For starters I eat, sleep, breathe for living." Chuckled Tanmay

Avi burst out laughing. "I guess somethings never change, felt my old buddy back".

"On a serious note, I do nothing for living, but I do a lot of things to live! Living comes following automatically." Replied Tanmay

"Otherwise, working as an illustrator, on a freelance basis. In simple words, I receive an idea from a client and then I put it in the shape of sketches, pictures, Maps, designs, etc. Work for some architects, some publishing houses, some editorials, some movie producers and as ghost to some illustrators as well. Have also assisted Gauri in one of her projects where she wanted some pictures to depict an evolution of some species she was working on while her short stay at some African country."

"Oh! Great! You always had a very good drawing hand. Seems good you followed your passion Tanmay and your love interest" winked Avi.

Tanmay blushed, "Well that is still a well-hidden secret', softly he said while looking at kids playing in the restaurant.

"Sometimes I feel Avi these birds are much freer than we humans are. We can learn so much from them".

Avi chose to remain quiet and gave space to Tanmay. He felt his sadness of unrequited love. Though he did want to know why he didn't tell her till now.

"So how do you feel drawing pictures and all?" After a while Avi tried to pierce the silence

"A picture is worth a thousand words", he replied while still being lost in his thoughts, sipping his coffee.

"You used to see people's Aura in the school. Colours and all-around people you used to see and tell how he or she is feeling that time. Do you still see it? Hey! How you see my Aura right now?", Avi asked it in excitement.

"We should keep some things to be talked about at Gauri's", Tanmay hushed him calmly.

"Right" Avi chose to keep mum now and enjoy his coffee.

They went on to take the flight to Goa. They were seating next to each other. Avi had this habit of listening to music while travelling. Tanmay was anyways engrossed in some book, so he took out his earphones and started to listen to some music. He glanced once to see the book he was reading. It had some geometrical figure on the cover page, like what he and Gauri was discussing the other day, that star of David. There was a big title of the book with the name of some English author, but all he could see or retain was this strange word in all other normal English words, was 'Merkabah'. There were some supernatural images on the cover page as well. He saw Tanmay engrossed in the book, so he plunged into his seat, closed his eyes, and started listening to some songs. He was carrying an MP3 player to listen, and it was in the midway where there were some bhajans and artis. He usually used to avoid it always, but somehow could not that time as there was this Mantra Chanting music which made him go a little trancey. His MP3 player showed the time of this mantra as 11:11 that is, eleven minutes and eleven seconds. He closed his eyes and started listening.

The music was in such a cadence, that he slowly went into a sleep like state where his head became like an empty vessel without a second thought. He drifted into deep slumber. In his sleep he started to see a strange vision. "What is that? Fire! Bon Fire! Linga, Tiger, no no, human, no half tiger half human. I have seen this before somewhere. What is he doing, who is he, this strange being." Avi felt bit scary but a strong urge to touch this strange being half tiger half human. He went ahead and touched him. He felt an immediate burst of energy coming to his body and then he saw his face. His heart started to flow and pounding faster at the same time. He saw him smiling at him and placed his hand on Avi's head. Avi tried to look more closely while sweating profusely. "What are you doing? Who are You?" Then he saw that linga.

It was a dense forest like place. Tall trees were all around, in between there was a large empty mud ground. It was a full moon night and there was a fire in centre of the ground and along with that a huge linga. A strong well-built man was there sitting, his face was like a fierce tiger while body was like half human. There were other animals too dancing along the fire like celebrating something. Tiger man was like their leader. The linga was not normal one. It was a huge uncarved linga which was being 'sthapit' at that place and that is why the celebrations were going on. He saw this half tiger half human reciting mantras around and started carving on that linga. One face, two face, he carved eight faces on that one linga in a symmetry. Four faces in the lower part and four on the upper. Wait! He has seen this linga before. "Pashupati Nath Ji?" He woke up almost gasping for breath. Tanmay rubbed his back seeing him in discomfort and gave him water to drink.

'What happened? You saw something?"

"Yes, Tanmay. I see some half tiger half human form from quite some time. He has appeared today third time in my dream when I was listening to some music. And I saw some strange things happening."

"Okay. Don't worry. Grasp your breath. It must have some connection with some of your past birth or something. Gauri is an expert in interpretating dreams. She has a gift, to see dream initiated lucid dreams and interpretating dreams of others. Let's discuss it with her, we are about to land anyway.", Tanmay said calmly.

Avi took some long breaths and had some water. He was calm by now. He saw outside from the window. Goa it is! Though this time Goa was not similar what it had been previously. He has always been to goa with his friends to enjoy the beach life, amazing discotheques, casino the night life and boozing. This time, there was an altogether different purpose. Something bigger was waiting for him and he could feel it.

***

They reached Gauri's in time. All three of them remembered the good old times, hugged each other in group, as they used to do in school. Remembering their last time, Gauri started singing, "We are the three best friends that...." and they laughed to the core.

Gauri had got prepared some awesome authentic Goan dishes for them. Gauri's house was beautiful. The vibes were so positive in her house that they both felt refreshed immediately. The tiredness was gone in seconds. She had kept it quite minimalistic, with simple cane furniture, wooden and mud shacks in her house vicinity, beautiful garden area with pebbles.

"Why you chose Goa to be your abode now? Your parental house was at Delhi, right?", Asked Avi inquisitively.

"Because this is where my Ajna Chakra got opened", Gauri said it with a sparkle in her eyes.

Avi saw Gauri amazed while Gauri and Tanmay saw each other and smiled at it. Sensing his confusion, Gauri spoke:

"Once I had come to Goa for some project of mine about two years ago. I used to come daily to this beach, used to sit by there for atleast two hours and just be. I used to sit there, for some time, just staring at the water, feeling the wind on my face. After a point of time, everything else around me used to fade, and there were only three things which were present in that very moment, Me, the winds, and the water along with its sound of crashing waves. This happened for a week or so. You can call it silent meditation by being in present moment. Water acted like as a magic to me, opening God knows what all inside me. One day as usual as I drifted in the moment, I became one with water slowly, as much, as there remained no difference after a point of time between water and my body. Water became me, and I, became water. The sound of water gushing became the music of life, the 'Anhad Naad' for me and I got lost in it like merged. That is when I felt strong sensations on my third eye and my eyes went half shut.

At that very moment, I saw very vividly, a strange royal blue colour circle in between my eyebrows with some strange designs and carvings inside it. It gave me strong sensations and vibrations, but it felt mystical, beautiful. Along with Ajna, Anahata chakra also started to flow, and it felt as if the energy is constantly rotating between Ajna and Anahata, like they also became one. I was walking like a druggie with no awareness where I am going, what I am doing. The whole day I could not talk to anyone properly. I was in such a state. I immediately went to my hotel room and slept. I slept for hours! When I woke up, the pain was still there though had receded, but it felt like something has changed inside me. Something got awakened and my senses got heightened. It was my first experience in opening of third eye or ajna. There are many more levels that comes in its full awakening, but it was the most important one. I meditated a little after waking up, tried to feel the oneness, which helped me to reduce my pain a little bit more. ", Gauri narrated everything as if it was happening just now.

Avi was listening to all this quite surprised. He was feeling so out of place listening to Gauri's and Tanmay's talks. He was also feeling quite small that time in front of them and inside his mind it was like how much they know things and how ignorant I am.

"Everyone starts from somewhere Avi. We all have been ignorant at some point of time. Being ignorant or blank is the first step towards marching to the spiritual journey", Tanmay Said.

"How did you know I was thinking about this right now?", Avi asked in shock.

"Could sense that", Tanmay winked.

"Okay. So, you guys were telling me that you want to tell me something about me. My reading and all. When are we doing it?" Avi asked.

"In some time when we shall reach the Agonda beach. Let's move!" Gauri said.

"Agonda? Never heard of this beach before", Avi asked Gauri.

"Yes! It is among the lesser famous beaches of Goa. Normally people flock around Calangute, Baga, Vagator etc, so this beach remains a little free. Plus, this is exactly where my third eye got opened", Gauri said it with winks.

They went to Agonda beach. It is in south goa and is quite pristine. There were no hawkers on the beach, and only a few people were there, mostly seeming to be locals who have their houses around or are owning the shacks on the beach and less visitors or tourists.

They walked on the beach for some time, enjoyed the nature. They sat there on some comfortable place and Gauri and Tanmay started meditating there. They were quite engrossed. Avi did not know what to do so he was just staring at waters or people passing by. He had long forgotten to understand or appreciate the beauty of nature.

After few minutes, they both opened their eyes and had a shine in their eyes. They strolled again and found a comfortable place under some roof where there was no direct sun light on them. It was windy and cool at that time especially since they were away from the direct sunlight.

Gauri asked Avi to share his things, what he has told her about his sorrows, pains, and all, so that Tanmay also can have a sense of it. He told everything, childhood things, his marriage things, his being so emotional and sensitive, his over compassionate nature etc. etc. While speaking he got tears in his eyes and stopped several times. Gauri encouraged him to still speak. Avi kept on saying things.

"So, this is all I had to say. About my life. The traumas and troubles I have been feeling. I cried a lot I know but don't know how, am feeling so much relaxed now. As if all that pain has been snatched away by some force. Feeling so happy and energised like all over again. I never felt this energy inside me, like from one year or so. I can climb mount Everest! What has happened to me? I have not felt this happiness inside from some time. Though I felt good vibes at your home, and we did laugh on things as well there, but this happiness was missing. What is this?", Avi was surprised, confused, amused all at the same time.

Gauri and Tanmay saw each other with smiles leaving Avi more confused.

'Well, before coming here in the shade, we were sitting on the shore meditating while you were looking around, right?", Asked Gauri

"Yes."

"Since then, we have been giving you 'Pranic Healing' ", Gauri said.

"What healing?", Avi was utterly confused.

"Let me explain that to you Avi. Prana is also called 'energy' or 'vital force' but that's a very rough translation. From the yogic point of view the entire cosmos is alive and breathing because of and with prana. The prana within all the created object creates the matter like human beings, plants, planets, asteroids, or a blade. Densities of Pranic energy particles varies in different permutation, and combination to create never ending matrix of creation. The core universal prana can be static or dynamic but it's behind the lowest to highest forms of existence.

On earth, the source of prana to sustain physical body of all living beings are air, food, water, and Sun. The air we breathe is very gross form of prana. However, the air we breathe is not prana as many yogis can survive without breathing. It's when prana leaves the body, death occurs. Prana can be categorised into universal or maha prana and individual prana. Maha prana can also be the kundalini energy lying latent in the Mooldhara (root chakra). Maha prana is also called the cosmic mother or para shakti, the first primal energy from unmanifested consciousness (para brahman) to trigger the creation in cosmos. This interaction of energy (prakriti) and consciousness (purusha) in each other is what is called cosmic play or 'Lila' and it causes creation or 'Srishti'. In Samkhya traditions prakriti is also referred to as Shakti and purusha as Shiv. When prana is stilled, kundalini rises and merges with consciousness in Ajna chakra (third eye).' Gauri tried to explain him.

"Have you ever observed how a stone statue of a deity, when first placed in your home temple, may seem dull and lifeless, but as you begin to pray to it, a beautiful and positive energy radiates from it? This is because the statue is infused with the power and energy, through the constant infusion of prana or energy, through chanting and pure devotional love. To your surprise, such a statue can even possess a finer prana or energy than that of a living human being. It is important to remember that non-living things should not be viewed as empty voids, as energy is always interacting with matter, both in living and non-living things. The only difference is that the frequency and quantum of prana in living beings is finer and stronger than in non-living things." Tanmay added.

"As individuals, our prana is a part of the universal prana, and until the veil is lifted, we see ourselves separate from the cosmic matrix. Through meditation, kriyas, and pranayama, we can become conscious of our own prana, which increases the existing quantum of prana. The prana is directed from the root chakra (Muladhara) to the third eye (Ajna), generating heat and increasing its frequency. The Healing we did to you was by channelling universal prana into our hands, with love, and transferring it to your individual prana, connecting your physical, mental, and emotional bodies. That is why you felt the way you did," said Gauri calmly.

"The energy is transferable. That is why we feel positive vibes at some places and negative vibes at others, as we discussed a little just now. We absorb the energies, at our own will. In some places we feel like rejuvenated while at some drained. I hope you have heard the name 'Energy Vampires'. When we meet certain people, we feel so much drained. Like they sucked our energy. It depends whether we are open to grab it or not. What you just feeling, is nothing but an energy transfer what we gave to you, fetching from the cosmos. We are just the mediums!", Tanmay explained it all with calmness.

"You also had a headache you were telling me while walking on the beach. Is it there now?", she asked further.

Avi was spell bound. He could not believe what he was listening to.

"Yes, the headache is gone. It was there and it was quite sharp before I started talking," Avi said, sounding amazed. "Is this like something from a movie or something?"

"It's because of the healing we gave you," Gauri explained.

"But this is just a temporary state, Avi. It's like giving air to a flat tire; you've inflated it again, but if you don't take care of it, it will deflate again one day," Tanmay added.

"But what can I do?" Avi asked.

"First step by identifying your blocks and its related sources. You got so many emotional and mental blocks, which are blocking the Chakras and thus affecting free flowing of prana in you, leading to these various health and anxiety issues in your body," said Gauri.

"But what is my fault, Gauri? What do you expect how would I be in my life circumstances Gauri," said defensive Avi.

"First step, stop being a victim. Second, have gratitude that you got this life. Everyone has got problems. Try to feel, compassion and love for the cosmos. Believe in their plan. Believe that everything that is happening is happening for a greater cause. And you are gifted Avi, I know you won't believe this today but one day you will get to know. Third, Practice Meditation and mindfulness, especially, Nadi Shodhan, Chakra Dhyanam, we will guide you on this. Fourth, cut the blocks, bondages, and ropes you have tied with your family. Like what Tanmay and I saw in your married life, you have four main ropes that is hampering you big time. You need to see them on your own, what they are and cut them so that the issues you are facing will perish. And last, but most important part Avi, Flow! Just Flow! That is your core, your strength.", said Gauri strongly.

Tanmay further added, "You think mine and Gauri's life has been easy? I am divorced after 6 years of marriage Avi but am happy since I chose my life over the societal bondage, and shackles. Gauri lost her grandmother three years back. If you remember she was very close to her since childhood. And there are many more things, that keep happening to us, physically, emotionally, and spiritually, but we face them with aplomb as we have attained a thing called 'Balance'. No one or nothing can have the power to control you. You are the driver of your own life. Your state of happiness and bliss depends on you and no one else. No One has that power Avi unless we give them that power.", Tanmay said bit sternly.

Avi gazed at Gauri, still unsure about the loss of her grandmother. But Gauri remained calm.

"Grand Ma had to go, and she's gone for her own good," Gauri began.

"She had completed the purpose of her life here. Although she had some blocks and attachments, especially to me, that's where I was able to help her 'pass over'. Her body had died, but her spirit was stuck at the gates of the earth. I talked to her spirit, consoled her, calmed her, and made her understand that we would be okay and there was no need to worry. She had a block related to her own father, which was difficult for her to overcome, but I helped her to release it. And that's how she was able to muster the courage to walk through the tunnel to her ancestral or spirit world."

Gauri spoke as if her grandmother had never left, as if she could still feel her, talk to her as vividly as when she was alive. It was as if she had overcome her fear of death completely, and it was just another ending for a new beginning.

"It's too much for me to process at the moment, to be honest," Avi said. "I also want to tell you about these dreams I've been having lately." Avi then shared with Gauri the dream or vision he had on the flight, about a half tiger and half human form.

Gauri closed her eyes for a few minutes before opening them again and saying, "That's your higher self, Avi. It wants you to connect with it. But let's talk about it later, as you're not quite ready yet. It will take some time to reach that stage, but you need to start now. Ask yourself, Avi, are you ready? Do you want to do this not for others, but for yourself? For your own soul journey and your own soul calling? Are you ready for the larger purpose that this life has for us, or do you just want to live a mundane life and must start again in the next?" Gauri asked Avi.

"I want to change myself Gauri. I want to. I will follow everything you have to offer. Please be my guides.", Avi asked them with folded hands.

Tanmay and Gauri hugged Avi. And started telling him about nadi shodhan and chakra dhyanam.

"Let me tell you briefly about Chakras, Nadis and how to remove the blocks. The Pranic body is fuelled by the Chakras which literally means "wheel "or circle, but according to yogic context, a better translation is subtle highly powered vortices of energy in the body. They act as transformers to distribute energies through Nadis to different organs in physical body as well as switch for illuminating higher dimension of consciousness in subtle bodies. Nadis simply means channels for the flow of energy. The rush of energy we experience during moments of exhilaration is through these channels. As our concentration goes deeper during meditation, we can trace the flow in form of vibrations.

Modern science explains it in the form of nerve impulses experienced in form of subtle flow of energy just like electricity, radio waves and laser beams.

According to tantras 72000 Nadis and much more, forms the networks in Pranmaya kosha (Energy Body) covering the whole frame through which the stimuli flow like an electric current. They are the pathways of Pranic, mental and spiritual currents providing energy to every organ & cell of the physical body. At psychic level they are perceived as rivers of light, colours, and sound while at physical level they are involved in all bodily functions and processes.

When a baby is born the Chakras and Nadis are not freely flowing, except few cases where because of some past life karmic shackles they are born with some diseases. Though I feel it's more of a lesson for the parents. As the kid grows, conditioning starts, this cycle of actions and reactions. If the frequency of thought and its associated emotions are high, it resonates with respective chakra frequency and prana flows freely leading to a healthy body. Though, if it resonates low the hindrance in channels develops. It is like we keep absorbing in so many low emotions in form of sadness, guilt, regrets, anger with no outlet. What happens if this happens in any water body? The water stagnates and start turning into muddy water, same happens in our body. Let me explain you more simply. For eg, if we lose someone or someone hurt us and we take it deeply, be victim, loose ourselves or self-love, bit selfish approach so blocks start happening in Anahata Chakra, and manifest in form of various heart diseases in physical body. Though if we have self-love, compassion, and put our consciousness in universal love, it flows freely."

"Ahh that's why yogis and saints hardly fall ill and have long life," said Avi excitedly.

"Yes Avi, now you are getting jest of it."

"So, all seven Chakras state depends on various low or high vibe emotions and respective blocks associated with it", asked Avi.

"Yes, Avi, though it's the first gate of balancing and opening it. Deeper we go, we can also tap into various psychic gifts associated with it"

"I see, so how should I start this, Gauri?", Avi asked.

"First of all, write down your blocks, weaknesses where you need working. Like what are your fears, pains, guilts etc. Next, we need to accept them. Then we start with yogic kriyas like first balancing Nadis and then Chakras. In chakra kriya we can start from mooladhara first, let go of its blocks and them move up. I can give you one chart too in which various Chakras and its respective blocks are present. That will help you to understand more."

"That will be of great help Gauri," beamed Avi.

"Let's stop today here only, you need time to process all of it. Let's head back".

As the three of them were heading back, Avi could feel the sand beneath his feet, its softness, like it was all there in front of him just he was not looking only. After a very long time the breeze that touched Avi cheeks bought a smile on his face.

Chapter 8

Dark And Light

> Without dark, there can be no light,
> Every soul pass through a dark night,
> They say, brightest of stars shine in darkest of night!

Next day, Tanmay woke Avi up for a meditation session. As they went out, they saw Gauri sitting on the beach wearing a breezy white floral dress. Her hairs were dancing and caressing her cheeks. Avi was like awestruck seeing so much serenity and glow radiating from her face. Tanmay was almost numb, Avi looked at him and teased him "So I am still wondering why you haven't told her yet".

"It's not the right time Avi" and he walked towards Gauri.

Gauri opened her eyes slowly, welcomed them, and told them to sit down. She first showed them a diagram of all Nadis and chakras and explained a bit about their location.

The 3 major nadis (rivers) and the 7 chakras (wheels of energy)

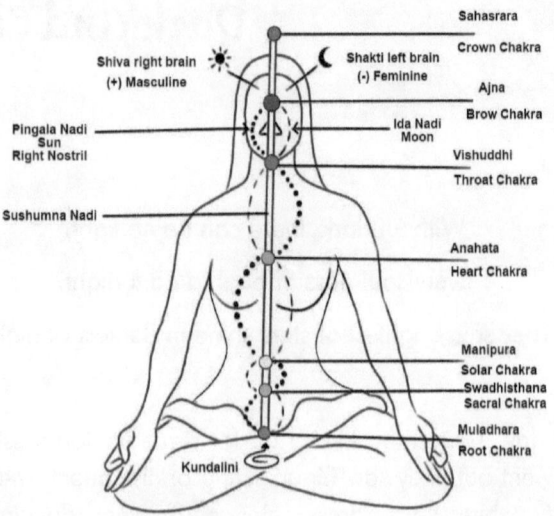

She told them to close their eyes and relax. She further continues and said, now please follow my voice.

First, do normal Anulom Vilom (Alternate Nostril Breathing) for around 10 full circles and observe the breath, as any thought comes let it come and go like a movie. Just observe the thoughts, do not become part of them.

Now, imagine the Sushumuna Nadi to be like string or thread while the chakras like pearls *on* it.

Then, bring your consciousness to Mooladhara Chakra, start with long deep breathing, inhale and feel white light along with your breath, going up to the Ajna chakra and retain breath there for as long as you can. Now as you exhale along with breath, feel white light back from Ajna chakra to Mooladhara. This is one full cycle. Repeat it for minimum ten times.

Now, as you become thoughtless bring your consciousness to Mooladhara chakra and feel red golden light coming from pure shakti (Primordial mother goddess) and removing your blocks of fear, survival crisis etc. Feel the power within you, trust in it, believe in it, you are the spark of the creator, nothing less, as you feel this power engulfing you. This is letting your blocks, which are getting removed in the form of black or grey energy, going out from your feet to mother earth.

As Next step, now, focus on tip of your nose also called nose tip gazing, as it amplifies further to balance root chakra.

Now bring your consciousness to centre of your eyebrows or Ajna chakra and just listen to the sound happening in the present moment, which is as of now the waves crashing the sea. Listen to it and slowly become one with it. Stay like this for ten minutes.

Now slowly rub your hand, keep it on your eyes and open it.

Avi was like, "Wow! what was that?" He was just beautifully numb, not able to speak anything. It was almost like he travelled deep to his soul and almost touched it. So much purity and tranquil he was feeling. He never felt like this ever before in his own life. It was like time has slowed down and he is diving deep into his own self. All humans have this potential to experience this ecstasy without any external stimuli of any addiction, but we choose to attract sorrows by getting stuck. It is all inside us and guess what no experience ever even came close to it. He was feeling so light like a bird like suddenly all the weight has been lifted off!

All he was able to utter two words looking at Gauri with utmost gratefulness 'Thank You'.

Avi's life changed after this meeting. He had started what Gauri and Tanmay had infused into him. He had found love in spirituality and meditation. It was an altogether new experience for him. He started following the process like a ritual. After he used to come back home from office, he used to sit in a comfortable half lotus sitting meditation pose (Sukhasana), as full lotus (Padamasana) was still out of his physical capabilities. At times he used to focus on all the chakras[3] one by one like Gauri taught him otherwise just focusing on one or two chakras throughout. She told him to focus on Mooladhara, the way she told, for minimum two weeks, then she will teach him how to let go of blocks of further chakras one by one. He used to focus on these for around half an hour, where he used to imagine the peculiar ball on each chakra with particular colour of that chakra, channelling from the pure divine source. He used to feel it revolving, as he felt pure colour along with good attributes related to that chakra, infused while inhaling and blocks getting out while exhaling.

Some days as he used to come to home and used to feel lot of negative energy taking a toll on him. At office even with so much work sometimes he used to feel fine but as soon as he used to step in home it was like hitting and draining. He knew something is not okay with energies at play because of his family negative traits. But this was hampering his growth. It was almost like he used to meditate and take one step further but like pushed back two steps because of it. He realised there was too much energy difference between him and them. Like he didn't belong there but for now he needed some solution to not let it hamper him. So, once he asked help from her how to protect and balance in such conditions. She told him about cleansing and shielding.

"How to do cleansing Gauri?" Avi enquired.

---

[3] For detailed knowledge about chakras please visit www.yogbhakti.me

"Avi when you sleep at night and you feel a lot of draining and tiredness without any reason, just know, you have been hit by rubbish energies. So, in cleansing, first take deep breaths become thoughtless and then channel white or golden divine light to each cell of your body. Feel it's concentration on every body part starting from your right-hand fingers to right shoulders, side of chest, going down to legs and right feet. Similarly do in left side and then go to back side of your body down from lower back to neck, head coming down to face. Then as you inhale, feel whole body bathing in this white light contracting and as you exhale feel whole body expanding. In the last step just free yourself and engross in the divine, while remembering the divine, feeling that love flow towards the divine and the cosmos, and just fly like a feather, swim like a straw, where there is no one else but just you in the whole cosmos. There is no body weight, nothing, as if melting and becoming one with the air. This is how you cleanse. It may take longer time, may be 40 minutes initially, but if you do daily, it may take much less time".

"Got it. And how to do shielding?" he asked

"While you do cleansing at night, before sleeping. After that you can shield too or it's best to shield in morning after chakra and silent meditation", She said calmly.

"Okay, how shielding helps us?" he asked with curiosity.

"It like creates a protective sheath or layer around you, to not let hit by any dark or negative energy, by people, intentionally or unintentionally."

"Unintentionally?"

"Yes, you know sometimes when we go to public places like parties, weddings, markets unknowingly sometimes we suck in rubbish energy. As you know like osmosis energy flow from high to low. In initial years of meditation this is very important because we are naïve and bit vulnerable as we start opening."

"Oh, I see. Makes sense. So, tell me how to do it!" he asked excitedly.

"Any God or source you connect with?"

"Oh, I connect with Shiva as you know".

"Oh yes, so imagine him up there, looking at you, smiling at you. Imagine strong force of white and blue light coming to you and making a balloon around you, covering you. Like in a round circle. There are much more advanced shields which you will channel on own as you advance in meditation, but this is like a basic one."

"That's interesting!"

"Do it daily, it will save you from unnecessary rubbish energies and you can conserve your prana to grow, than, fighting them off"

"Yes, I get it" he said confidently. "Thank you", he obliged.

So, in morning he used to meditate, do yogic kriyas and shield himself. And in night he used to cleanse himself and listened to music. His body initially started showing weird signs. He started having breathlessness, cough, and mucus at times with sniffles, loose motions, Diarrhoea, Nausea, flatulence, fever, Headaches and what not. He was confused like what is happening with him. Should not he be getting better and feel nice after all these pranayama and meditation. Why suddenly he is getting all these symptoms. One day when it became unbearable, he called up Tanmay.

"Tanmay bro!!!"

"What happened Rana Avi!", Tanmay Chuckled at his broken voice.

"Don't laugh you dolt!"

"Okay Okay. What happened to Mr. Avi?", Tanmay still was not able to control his laughter but tried hard to suppress as he could understand why he has this kind of voice.

"I am having an uncontrolled poop, You nincompoop!!!", Avi said.

Tanmay laughed like anything, though Avi was irritated, first because of his condition and then this laugh of Tanmay, but he could not control but laugh.

"Can understand!"

"What can you understand? I don't know what I should do! I don't want to see a doctor for this!"

"Don't go to a doctor for this! Coz this is not something a medical condition you are going through."

"As in?"

"When we step on this spiritual journey when we try to work on our chakras, try to settle our karmas and blocks, these old blocks which are accumulated since long, tries to find its way to go out of our system. You may experience a sudden increase in your mucus generation, this what you are observing in the form of diarrhoea, at times feels like to throw up, gastric things and alike. Even Fever can be a medium to let these blocks go."

"You are right! I am experiencing almost all the things with me. Sometimes it is just one symptom and at times it is like everything happening at the same time. "

"Now you know it. It is perfectly fine. Let it go out of your system. And don't worry, this will not last forever. You are not going to roam around places shitting your pants!"

Avi said nothing but "huhhh!"

"Haha. These symptoms will go away slowly till you find a little balance and these blocks go out. I know it pains a little that time, irritates us, frustrates us. But Avi, See the positive side. These signs means that you are growing! That the age-old blocks are finally going out. Every darkness brings with it the promise of a new sunrise, the light! Isn't it a happy satisfying feeling to know that we are indeed progressing in our spiritual journey, a little by little. See it as a purification process which needs an outlet to go.", Tanmay said it with poise and smiles on his face.

"Getting it Tanmay", Avi returned with smiles.

"The important thing is, don't control it. Like if you are getting mucus, let it go out. Let the blocks go! And not even by mistake eat any medicine. They supress it, you may feel relief temporary, but they again come back. They only worsen the whole process. I believe every disease is because of some underlying blocks which can be healed by going deep into root cause core and letting it go. If you take medicine, they never get out and only worsen the condition. Me and Gauri have not taken a single medicine, unnecessarily, since we started meditation, been years and we are alive!!", he beamed.

"Aye Aye captain!"

Avi has been doing all the meditation techniques he had learnt so far, plus was also reading spiritual books, some good quotes, and was following the spiritual podcasts. Even at office he used to take some time out to just sit in silence for few minutes, thoughtless with eyes closed focusing on his third eye. Slowly, Slowly, he had started liking the process. He used to ask every now and then to both Gauri and Tanmay, how his chakras are looking. What does his Aura signifying and getting satisfaction like a child when there is a positive change in his Aura or his Chakra more balanced. Balance of yin and yang, dark and light within our own selves. He had cut off from most of his friends he didn't connect with. At home too he used to now spend less time with family and more time with his own self. Slowly he started to feel unaffected and neutral with everyone. They were losing control and power over him. He could see the insecure patterns of Malvika too. He had distance himself physically and emotionally from her. She used to try to come close to him, sometimes seduce him, but he just used to ward her off. He just couldn't feel any connect and lot of resistance. Almost like his instincts were being confirmed that she felt many things but never that pure love and only wanted to bind and own him. His communication, expressing his truth, taking stands for what is right reached a new level at home, office, in friends, which earlier he used to avoid or suppress. His connects were decreasing, addictions were almost now zero, his weight had reduced, everyone around him were quite surprised seeing his new version. He himself was!!

Until one day, when he became badly indisposed.

***

Avi felt a strange fever once when he was at office. It was as if someone was throwing fire at his face. He literally felt as if he is sitting near to a volcano and facing all the heat of the lava flowing even in the cold AC office. He was perfectly fine till then, no signs of temperature or nothing and suddenly he started feeling these. As if someone exhaling these fumes on his face. Simultaneously he also felt banging on head. Like someone hammering his head out of nowhere. He felt a little giddy, removed his spectacles, and sat with his head down on the desk.

He stayed like this for some time, but he still was feeling that heat and banging. It had been two hours; he got a severe headache and fever along. He could not understand what is happening, he was totally fine in morning no cough or cold and suddenly this! In his heart he remembered Gauri, like please help me and suddenly he got a ping on his phone. It was Gauri! Woah is it telepathy or what he pondered!

"Hey Avi. Been some days, I got a strong feel you are not okay, how are you? "

"Gauri!! Can I call you now?"

"Sure Avi"

Avi called her.

"Gauri. Don't know but am feeling a lot of heat on my face as if some dragon is exhaling fumes over my face. My head is also banging like crazy, I never felt anything like this before!"

"What? Since when? And how is your health? You sound so down!"

"It has been two hours. I am feeling so feverish and have such a heavy headache can't tell you."

"Why did not you tell me before you fool! Wait! Lemme check!"

The phone went silent for some time and after a few moments Gauri spoke again.

"Avi. Close your eyes and feel. Just feel and nothing else. Okay?"

"Okay"

Avi tried to feel as Gauri had told. For few seconds he could feel nothing, then after a while he felt little sensations on his wrist, then his face, then his legs, and his head. It was as if someone was touching him. Slowly his fever went a little down and his headache too came down. He suddenly felt as if someone held his face in hands. It was strange! But he felt good! He was feeling better, getting better. After few minutes he was almost like how he was feeling before that strange fuming feeling.

"How are you now Avi?"

"I am feeling better Gauri. Thanks! You healed right?"

"We! Me and Tanmay. He has been also there to heal you. We had come to you astrally and healed you since it was not a normal thing. You were under attack Avi!"

"Attack what? How it is possible and who will attack me? I don't see anyone around me" he panicked.

"It is not physical attack Avi, it's spiritual one."

Avi zoned out. Gauri shook him a little and continued.

"Avi, you cannot see energy, but it is there, and we feel it just like that. There are dark spirits too. Where there is light there is darkness too. It is okay. Don't panic! In this journey it happens but don't make a big deal out of it. Let's focus on who did it, why and how to defend in future. We tried to find the source of it by tracing down the spirit, but we could not. Feels like some strong spirit it is or it is into dark magic. But we both had this strong feeling that it was someone you are quite close to and have given extreme power to. Otherwise, this nature of attack is impossible since you are growing well."

"What are you talking about?", Avi was confused, concerned, panicked all in that moment.

"See. Suppose your phone is drained out of battery and it is connected to charger which is inserted in the socket. But the switch is not on, will it get charged?"

"No, obviously!"

"But why? The Charger is connected, then why it is not getting charged?"

"Coz the switch is off. There is no power transmitting to it that is why. What are you trying to say Gauri?"

"Exactly my boy! When there is no power, there will be no action. Only when power is given, the action happens. In your case, the attack has happened this strong only since you have given power to some person or spirit, because of some thread of attachments with him or her as you were also shielded".

"Yeah! Had created a shield around me this morning."

"Yes. Plus, me and Tanmay has also been taking care of your shield daily. Since you are a beginner, your shield is a little weak. We raise your shield daily and try to create a Merkabah around you!"

"Merkabah? Had heard or seen this word before somewhere. Anyways. What now?"

"You need to see this on your own. How you got this attack and all. And who made it."

"What about these sensations I felt? It was like magical, one moment I was feeling like I am in hell and next moment it just calmed down almost by 70%"

"Yes, we healed you by coming to you astrally, as I just said. Healing is not only done by being physically near but also through distance like this. Energy is not bound to time and space, this even now science have started to take into consideration. Now you know how. Our spirits came to you, not soul. Though some advanced yogis also have sidhhi or gift where their soul leave their body completely, that's like full astral projection, what we did is like partial one to help you."

"But how did you heal me so vividly, it was almost like someone held my face for real".

"Yeah. It was me! Could not see you in that much pain. Don't know, but at times I get such motherly vibes for you, can't even explain. As if you are my soul baby. Just could not stop myself to caress your face and like saying to you, don't worry, things will be fine. With this pure love, I channelled healing energy and light and gave to you." said Gauri with so much love and concern.

"Awww! Gauri! Can understand that. Have felt so much of respect for you as well, like always. You remember in our school times once I had touched your feet?"

"Oh yeah! I just got remembered! There can be something to it Avi. It just cannot be a coincidence that there is this devotion in you for me."

"How do you feel now?" she further asked.

"I feel much better now".

"Take some rest. We will figure about the source of attack later."

"Ok thank you so much Guru Maa", he laughed.

Gauri and Tanmay had a conversation about attack that night. They both were concerned about Avi.

"What did you see Tanmay?" she asked.

"I saw two black spirits attacking him, they were quite strong and powerful. They were literally sucking his energy and like kind of trying to hypnotise him for certain things. Like someone wanting to control him and being furious for him going away."

"Yes, even I felt the same. It was quite dark and not any random attack. I felt dark magic".

"What is the difference between normal spiritual attack and dark magic?" he asked curiously.

"Well, there is a lot of hype around it, I know, especially in our country. But to be honest it is nothing but doing certain stuff with wrong intents, fuelled by jealousy, selfishness to have control or power. It is like chanting even normal mantra and praying or even strongly thinking about someone but with wrong intents. Those thoughts go into the cosmos and dark spirits help it to manifest it because they feed on such virtues. It is more powerful because it usually done by closed one whom we have given power to like some family member, friend and sometimes an enemy. Hating someone is also like giving him or her power. Sometimes help is also taken through a strong dark spiritual human or even force just like we take from divine force. Light and dark all part of cosmos. While in normal spiritual attacks it's like some spirits getting attracted to growing light and power in some spiritual aspirants. It's easier to nullify them as compared to dark magic and now you know why. It's a wrong belief that there are skulls, tantrik and all involved in dark magic, like you know, always. It does happen that way as well, but not always. Any human whose consciousness is constantly involved in emotions, opposite to love, compassion, oneness keeps getting more and more dark enough to manifest it and harm someone through various medium. At the end it is all an energy game! And they receive power too, like we do, though from opposite source. So, any wrong evil thought directed to someone through chants or prayers, or energy is, sub consciously, a dark magic as it has the same or similar effect of what tantrik dark magic has. But know, love has got all the power to transform darkness!"

"Well, that's a new insight, for sure".

"The magic of a mother's cooking is undeniable, isn't it, Tanmay? The love and care that goes into preparing a meal can elevate it to something truly nourishing for the soul. But even the same dish can lack that same energy when it's made by someone else. It's all in the intent and energy behind it. And let's not even get started on food made with negative thoughts and emotions. It's truly mind-blowing how much of a difference it can make."

"I completely agree, Gauri. I remember when my mom makes my favorite dish, Rajma Chawal, I could eat plate after plate. But when I get it from a restaurant, it just doesn't have the same satisfying effect. But then, there are some restaurants where I do feel satisfied, not just because of the taste, but the pranic value you mention. It just goes to show how powerful the intent and energy behind a meal can be."

"Exactly, Tanmay. It's not just a product to them, but something they're offering to someone with love and care. The intent and energy truly make all the difference."

"But what if there is a necessity to eat outside food because of unavoidable circumstances, like trips and all in that case how to ensure its pranic value?" asked Tanmay

"Well in that case we can always clean the food before eating. You can close your eyes and visualize white, or baby pink pure light being infused in the food and cleaning it from any lesser form of energy, likewise we can clean it. That is the reason behind why in so many cultures we pray to God before eating, as we pray, we somehow channel positive energy of gratitude into food. If we can understand there is a logical reason behind all the practices that have been done since ages. Only if we try to dig deep" replied Gauri.

"So true! But Gauri, our friend can be in danger. We must help him to figure then in case some closed one is involved".

"Yes, let us do it tomorrow."

The next day, Gauri called Avi to know how he is feeling. She also had to help him to see the source of the attack.

"Hello Avi. How are you, dear?", She asked with lot of concern.

"I am better Gauri. Just finished a meditation session".

"Oh Great. So, let me help you now to look deeply into, what exactly happened yesterday. Close your eyes, I am helping you open your Ajna chakra and Anahata chakra more so that you can see and feel more clearly and strongly." She said excitedly.

"Okay Gauri, but how will I know what I am seeing is right and not a figment of mind's imagination."

"Well, imagination can only be done to the extent where in you have seen or heard things in your life and stored them in your conscious memory. How can you imagine something you never saw or even thought about it ever? As our Ajna chakra opens and get balanced more and more, we can tune into a higher frequency and can see the unseen. It is like our spiritual antennae. If our heart chakra flows when we see something deeply or read someone, means, we are seeing right. it is like an indicator. That is my experience".

"Okay let me try then", Avi closed his eyes and started to see deeply as Gauri opened his chakras more. He felt a lot of pressure in between his eyebrows and suddenly saw a glimpse of a woman behind the attack with dark red and black aura around her. As he was about to open his eyes suddenly, he also saw a man with a dark purple Aura. He started to breathe very heavily. Gauri calmed him down by grounding him. He slowly opened his eyes.

"Are you okay Avi? What you saw?" she asked

In a trembling voice he said, 'I saw a woman and a man, Gauri..' and then he stopped

"What? Tell me Avi!"

"I strongly felt the energy of woman to be that of Malvika!" he was shaking. "Maybe I saw wrong Gauri, can you please confirm?"

"Did your heart flow?"

"Yes! Like very strongly"

"Then you are not wrong, trust it. It's okay. Life is full of surprises. What we see often is not true and what we don't see is the truth! We are blinded by attachments and illusions".

"But she into dark spirits and attacks how is it possible? She is my wife for God's sake." He suddenly didn't know whom to be angry at, himself or Malvika or cosmos.

"Calm down dear, it's okay. Darkness and light, both are part of us. We all have Sattvic, Rajsic and Tamsic Guna. In some humans one of the guna proportions is higher than other and vice versa. In some, the tamsic insecurities, obsession reach such threshold that their spirit unknowingly or knowingly channels darker spirits, forces and initiate such attacks. May be Malvika spirit got more darker as she started to feel resistance from your energy and losing control over you. Her deeply buried gifts and powers may be from some birth sadhna awakened with high rage as she started to lose control over you. Either she is intentionally taking help of some guru for all this what we call as tantriks or even her human self doesn't know that her raging negative emotions are making her so dark that she is becoming source of dark attacks on her own husband. But one thing is sure her spirit is quite powerful; she is obsessed for you and there is past life karma connect. Nothing happens randomly. You also mentioned a man with purple aura, I guess this puzzle can only be solved by going to associated past life through past life regression therapy"

Suddenly like a vision flashed before his eyes and he said "Gauri with this I remember that dream I got, the path where there was so much darkness and fire and Malvika was there. Oh God! It all makes so much sense now. I decoded it so wrong, it was that she is dark still you wanted to choose it, because it seemed like a shortcut to reach somewhere, like home. I thought Malvika was there to help me but.. Shit! What have I done with my life!"

"You have chosen right Avi. Remember, BRIGHTEST OF STARS SHINE IN DARKEST OF NIGHT. In a way you will learn a lot and grow tremendously with all these obstacles and reach your true home. For now, let's plan to meet at Delhi, can't make you do PRT on call alone, it's not safe."

'Okay! Give me some time to plan this out. I know it's important to see. Will catch you soon."

Avi's mind was a jumbled mess as he made his way to Delhi. He couldn't understand why Malvika would do something so heinous. What had he done to deserve such a tragic fate in his life? Why had he been so blind to the signs and warnings that Tara had given him? He couldn't shake off the feeling of guilt for not being able to protect her.

He thought of Tara, his true love, and a tear rolled down his face. "Where are you, Tara?" he whispered. "All I wanted was a connection like we had before, but now I feel so far from it." He knew that he needed to find a way to come to terms with the past and move on, but the weight of his guilt and sorrow was heavy on his heart. He just hoped that he would find the answers he needed during his weekend in Delhi.

At one side chaos was going on inside him but at the same time he was little bit excited too. He had been so passionate about this when he had first learnt it from Gauri. "You have done PRT on your own?', Avi had jumped saying this. PRT stands for past life regression therapy, where the blocks or issues from past lives are removed by some trained practitioner/ psychologist or hypnotist. Gauri had done it on her own without taking any external technical help by going into her past. When her Ajna chakra opened, she tapped into this gift of time travel. She not only could see her own timelines but also of other people. She was truly blessed with this divine gift of time. She often used to say it's because her core element is that of water and 'WATER REMEMBERS'. She had shared a lot of things about that with Avi and had also told him the precautions and warnings attached to it as it requires a lot of emotional stability and divine protection otherwise the spirit can even get stuck at some birth. Everything has its own pros and cons.

"So, our dear Manulal have been busy, fighting spirits and all?", teased Tanmay.

"Yo bro! But what is all this man? Never even imagined in my wildest of dreams about all this"

"HaHa! welcome to the party my boy"

"You bet!"

Soon Gauri started the procedure and asked him to lie down comfortably, loosening his body.

"As I will take you into your past birth, your spirit will slowly deep delve into it."

"Gauri before you start can I ask something?"

"Sure"

"What is the difference between spirit and soul?"

"Good question actually! For the longest of time, even I was confused about it. Think of it like a fruit," Gauri began. "The seed represents the soul, the pulp represents the spirit, and the energy that gives it life and allows it to grow, change colour, develop flavour and aroma, is like the pranic energy. We, as humans, are also made up of these three elements: the soul, spirit, and energy, or atman, purusha, and prakriti. The soul, or superconscious, is always pure and guides us towards what is right and divine. It's the spirit, or subconscious, that goes through the cycles of birth and death, and can be influenced by darkness or light depending on its interaction with the pranic energy, or consciousness.

It's this interaction that governs our births, driven by our karmic seeds, lessons and the three virtues."

"So, it will be my spirit fuelled by prana that will now travel and not soul".

"Only very high-level yogis have capability to let soul leave the body and come back, though it's not safe at all. Body is like an empty vessel and without soul any spirit can possess it. I will also shield you in this procedure too so that you don't bring back any rubbish energy from there".

"But why can't you see my past birth Gauri, I know you have that gift to see."

"I can see Avi, but it is not righteous to see someone else's past lives. It is like interfering with the timelines. And see, I can guide someone to see theirs by helping them open their chakras a little for a while, but not right to see on their behalf. This is something one should do on own."

"Help me then to see them!"

"Ready Avi?"

"Yes, Gauri. Tell me what to do."

"I can feel your energies. They look good. You can be taken to your past birth. First, shield yourself and then take 10 long deep breaths and go thoughtless. Then just follow what I tell you. Okay?"

"Okay"

Avi followed what Gauri said and slowly went into near to thoughtless state. And sat silently and comfortably focusing on the Ajna.

"Avi! You are in a deep hypnotic state. You know that you are going to feel and live the most amazing moments of your life. Your spirit shall be travelling into astral realms and will reach that birth which you want to see. You are an old soul and had lots of births on earth. Ask your spirit guides or Shiva, to take you to that birth which you need to see the most for understanding your spiritual journey and its lessons. Ask them, why you took birth, chose your current family, what are your major lessons and why this darkness. Ask them to take you there smoothly and show you everything you need to know. At the end, show them your gratitude and with utmost respect, take your spirit back to your body. You are ready?"

"Yes. I am"

"Okay. On the count of three, your spirit shall leave for travel into astral plains. Let it flow freely to that birth, which you need to see. There is a door and on my count of One, Two, three, you will open it!!!"

Three, two and one!!

There was a silence for some seconds. Gauri knew what is happening with him. She was cautious too and had shielded him well.

"Where do you see yourself Avi?"

"I am seeing a road, like a village. There is very less greenery, and I am sitting with someone under a tree. I am wearing white dhoti kurta and a white head gear like what a village person wears. Though it is a little muddy due to regular wear and tear. There is this bicycle, that black coloured one, the old kind of. I have been riding it along with this lady with whom I am sitting."

"Who is that girl? Can you recognise her from the present birth. See her eyes. Face can change but eyes are window to soul. What era is this?

After a brief pause, he continued.

"It looks like pre independent India era, like early 1920's or something. The roads are not developed that much. A small concrete road it is and is not very robust the way it is now a days. This lady, I am feeling a very close close feeling with her. There is so much love I can feel in both. Not being able to see her properly though. But the love is so pure and beautiful." Suddenly Avi started feeling sweat around his neck, under his ears. He became a little uncomfortable. Gauri could sense his discomfort, through his energies as well as his short breaths. Without wasting the time much, she asked again.

'Who is she Avi?"

"Tara!"

"Who is Tara?"

Avi could not speak so Gauri changed the direction, though she could understand bits of it.

"Ask Tara to take you to a place where the foundation of these present circumstances happened".

"She has taken me to some huts, small huts of mud. There is a small colony, with no roads whatsoever. There are some five huts in a row and farmlands in front. Like equal portions of farmlands outside each hut. There is a small muddy road between every two farms, enough for walking or for a bicycle to travel only. There is a water well outside my hut and an open kitchen. Tara and I are married. Beautiful life we have and three kids, two girls and one boy. We spent some beautiful times together in this house, at farmland and around the village. The place seems to be from Rajasthan. I have big moustache and Tara is in some simple lehenga choli dress. We are living a simple, happy and content life together. I am lying on her laps under the tree, in the farmlands. She brings food for me there as lunch, some plain chapatis, green chillies and onions with salt. We are taking food together and seeing each other with so much of love. Sprinkling water at each other."

"What else can you see?"

"Tara!!!" he shrieked.

"What happened Avi?" Gauri held his hands,

"She is not well. She is vomiting blood. She is in so much pain." he said with so much pain like it's all happening right now.

"What is her age? And why is she feeling this pain and all. Ask her. Try to see the complete picture, Avi."

A silence remained for few seconds.

"She is dying!!" Avi said with a heavy voice and uncontrollable tears trickling down from his eyes.

"Why? And what age she is in?"

"In her late thirties. She ate something which was not good, and she is lying there like that. I am so helpless and crying. The local doctor is trying to make her conscious, but she is losing it. She is looking at me and the kids with all that pain and smiling with tears, like a compassionate smile with lots of emotions flowing".

"Go deep Avi. Why she ate something like this?"

A silent was ablaze again. After a few seconds, Avi spoke again.

"She has been poisoned!"

"What? Who did that Avi?" she asked calmly yet putting slight pressure on him.

"Malvika!" he trembled.

"Why she did that?"

"I don't know".

"I am holding your hand Avi, don't be afraid. You are protected. You must be strong to see everything to understand the complete picture. You want to know right why Tara had this tragic end? Isn't it? Muster courage my dear. Stay there. See, feel, why it all happened. Don't lose!" she remained composed,

"Okay!"

Avi fell silent once more. Gauri felt uneasy. She had seen her previous lives and had witnessed the deaths of loved ones, but she had never seen someone kill or murder someone. She waited patiently for Avi to continue.

"I saw," Avi began.

"What did you see Avi?" Gauri prompted.

"Malvika stayed close to our home as a servant to one of the farmland owners. I saw her wearing a black Rajasthani dress with some silver jewellery and black dots on her face, part of her makeup. Her family were landless farmers who had lost their land and possessions and were working on other's land to earn a living. They were looked down upon by the locals. Malvika had a liking for me, but Tara and I were together since childhood. This created a turmoil in her mind, and she became obsessed with having me, wanting to live a better life because I had more monetary privileges. She started praying differently. Her aunt, who lived with her, helped her. The intent of her chants was to take me and somehow live with me. Over the years, she grew stronger because she was very dedicated in her approach. Every night she would chant mantras and do some dark rituals to please other forces. Initially, it didn't affect us because even Tara was not an ordinary woman. Her love and dedication for her family was so pure that it unknowingly created a shield around us, protecting us from any kind of darkness. All Malvika's tricks and gimmicks failed because of Tara's high spiritual energy. She tried many times to make mine and Tara's life a living hell by manipulating her about me and me through my friends by hypnotizing them and telling them what to do. But since we loved each other and Tara's energy was high, she couldn't do much harm. Tara had warned me about Malvika's intentions many times, but I, like a fool, never paid heed to her. I was like a blind man living in a fool's paradise under Tara's protective wings, unaware of how dangerous things were getting. 'I don't believe in all this stuff, we are living happily, why do you keep bringing this nonsense up again and again? I know her since my childhood, why would she harm us? I can't tell her to stop coming to our home. Look how our children adore her, maybe you are being insecure.' Heartbroken, Tara had no other option but to single-handedly fight the darkness that Malvika brought, which she did like a lioness. This made Malvika even more furious and one day she crossed all her limits."

"What happened then Avi?" Gauri asked with a sense of dread.

"One day, she came to Tara and... "

Avi stopped and had short breaths. Gauri could not break this flow and there was a little time as Avi was not that strong enough at present to be able to be in this hypnosis long.

"What then Avi?

"She threatened Tara with her powers. She roared with bloodshot eyes 'If you don't back off, I will do terrible things with your kids and husband, you can't even imagine. You won't be protecting them day and night. Your husband doesn't even believe you, that is the biggest loophole that will one day give me an upper edge,' she laughed wickedly.

She showed Tara how her powers were becoming stronger enough to harm the family because of this loophole. Tara is terrified and pleaded with her to leave them. Malvika told her she will not even touch her family and may also take care of them, only if she chooses to go away. She must die! Tara, being Tara, could not even imagine something happening to her family and was willing to sacrifice herself for their safety, though she was sad only if Avi would have believed her and helped her this all wouldn't be this tragic.

"According to part of the plan, Malvika gave her some oranges to eat which she had infused with dark powers enough to take one's life. Tara saw her kids for the last time, hugged them, cried with loud sobs, and went out and ate those oranges. She fell on the ground immediately and Malvika called everyone to the scene, enacted playing innocent cards. Malvika was sobbing with crocodile tears, manipulating everyone by showing her deepest concerns and bringing the local doctor along, knowing fully that no one can do anything now. She used all the dark powers she had accumulated over the years to murder Tara in cold blood. I was not there, I was working and when I came back, I found her lying in a pool of blood. I couldn't believe what had happened. No one knew it was Malvika who did it. I went running to Tara, and lay her head on my lap, we are crying seeing each other like hell, and then, in no time, her soul left her body and she lay dying in my lap. She did not say a word to me. I was in shock; my whole world had crumbled. I was devastated, lost, and alone." Avi's voice broke as he spoke, tears streaming down his face.

Gauri held his hands, consoling him and urging him to look further.

"Then what happened Avi?"

"Then Malvika moved in with us. The kids had already grown close to her even before Tara was murdered. It was part of her plan, and like a fool, I allowed her to stay in my home because I wanted someone to take care of the kids in my state of mind and I did not know that it was her who killed Tara. Many times, I remembered what Tara told me about her, but I was so consumed by my grief over losing her that I couldn't hear that voice. After about ten years or so, consumed by memories of Tara and the depression of losing the love of my life, I too gave up my life to a disease," Avi's voice cracked.

"Okay Avi, now bring your consciousness back to the present slowly. Come back to the gates of this birth, and on the count of three, leave everyone and everything behind and come back. Release everything there! Be grateful to the cosmos and your divine guides for helping you through this. Now, on the count of three, come back. One, two, three!"

Avi returned to the present. He felt a sharp pain in his third eye, but he was barely aware of it. He was crying like a child, unable to believe what he had just seen. Gauri and Tanmay urged him to drink some water, catch his breath, and calm down. Tanmay was also deeply shaken, having never experienced anything like this in his spiritual journey or any of his past lives.

"I'm sorry Avi," Gauri said, tears welling up in her own eyes. "I know it's hard to process, but you need to let go of this pain, it's holding you back. You need to forgive Malvika and yourself for not being able to protect Tara. You need to move on and live your life, for Tara, for yourself, and for the ones who love you."

Avi nodded, wiping his tears. He knew that Gauri was right, it was time for him to let go and move forward.

"It was all in the past Avi! Nothing in present. But you know now, how it is all related to our present. There are a lot of karmic relations we form Avi to learn the lessons. We need to learn those lessons and move ahead towards our growth and journey. Your dissatisfaction in your married life has a major reason for this past birth of yours. I guess, you know it well and I don't have to tell you more.'

"Gauri... Tanmay... I let my Tara murderer stay with me and our kids!! If only I had listened to her, she wouldn't have died such a tragic death. I am the one responsible for this, I deserved every bit of pain and suffering I felt in this life" and he burst out crying heavily.

Tanmay hugged him and Gauri caressed his back. They stayed like that as if all three were feeling that agony with tearful eyes.

After some time, Gauri told Tanmay to drive him back as he was still not in his senses. 'It will be all fine Avi, you take a rest, and we will meet again tomorrow to discuss it and Tara' she winked and smiled, trying to console Avi.

Gauri started alone to her hotel room. She was also a bit shaken by all that she witnessed. In her life also she had a close one who did dark tricks on her, but she subconsciously or consciously always fought it. It was this experience that heightened her gift to tackle and neutralise darkness. She also sensed lord Shiva and Shyam (Lord Krishna) divine protection with her. As she was heading back in the taxi, she felt something strange for seconds. But she was so lost in

Avi's experiences, she didn't pay heed. She got back to her hotel room, freshened up and retired to sleep. Suddenly, she felt goosebumps on her skin, and she knew some spirit is there. As she tried to visualise who is there in no time, the centre of her head started to pain resolutely. It felt as if the spirit is banging bricks on her head, she started to feel dizzy as she held her head. It was an unbearable torment, as she also started to feel very weak like being sucked. She cried in pain and with great difficulty pinged both Avi and Tanmay, that she needs help. Her eyes were going blurry and losing grip on the phone. She tried to channel her energy and ward it off but to no avail. Whomever this force was, it was very powerful nothing like she ever encountered before.

There, Avi and Tanmay read her message. They tried calling her and messaging her but to no avail. Tanmay then called Avi and said, 'We need to rush there, I feel she is under massive attack'. They both anxiously sprinted to her hotel room. Holding her head all blurry she opened the door and fell in Avi's arms.

"Gauri!!" she was shaking, and they made her lie on the bed. Tanmay immediately raised shields of him, Avi and Gauri and instructed Avi to keep calm and along with him close his eyes and try to see what was happening.

"What do you see Avi?"

"I saw a spirit with purple aura, wait, Tanmay! He is the same, as I saw in my vision!! Mr. Purple!"

"Yes, even I can see him, and he is not alone, I see Malvika's spirit too along with him and the whole army. They are like constantly attacking Gauri, sucking her energy".

"How to stop them Tanmay, I will help", Avi said fiercely. Tanmay glanced at Avi, who was suddenly radiating intense energies because of what he saw happening with Gauri.

When we see pain of the loved ones, we can go to any extent to help, was buzzing in Tanmay's head.

"We will close our eyes, become thoughtless and channel powers from our higher selves along with our spirit guides guidance".

They started to go deep and since they both were emotionally so enraged seeing Gauri's state like this, it made them push their own limits to channel strong power from the cosmos. Tanmay anchored a trident from his higher self, that was given by Lord Shiva in one of his past ancient births. While Avi felt Pashupati Nath Ji giving him a sword with big gems. While Avi took care of the army, Tanmay dealt with Malvika and Mr Purple. He touched their spirit with a trident, blocking their powers. In the meanwhile, Gauri also woke up a little unconscious as she started to feel a bit better since now the powers of those spirits were blocked off.

Tanmay and Avi shouted at him 'Why are you attacking her?'

Mr. Purple glared at Gauri and bellowed, "Because she's interfering with our plans. Avi belongs to Malvika, and you have no right to take him away from her grasp. She's worked so hard to get him for so many lifetimes."

Gauri smiled serenely and replied, "We are all children of the creator, no one can own anyone. He has suffered enough, I will never leave his side no matter what, and one day he will be free from this dark cycle."

Mr. Purple snarled, "You foolish woman! Do you even know who you're messing with? Why are you determined to repeat history again? This time, he won't leave you, not after what you did to him eons ago."

The three of them were flabbergasted, they had no idea what he was talking about.

"What are you saying?" Gauri asked, completely bewildered.

"Hahaha! You humans, you don't remember anything from your countless past lives. I feel so sorry for you all," Mr. Purple sneered.

He approached Gauri and whispered, "Your ancient battle as a goddess with the demon king. The king, who is the fiercest of them all. He, who is the greatest slayer of all. He, who even the demigods are afraid of. He, who is the emperor of darkness. He, who is tall as a mountain and strong as a rock. He, whose name alone strikes fear into the hearts of mortals. He, who is my Guru. The ruler of this age, the mighty Kali! He's back, as the age is ending, and he won't let you succeed."

"तमः वर्धतु!!"

Chapter 9

Pearls Of Gauri

The destination is one, though roads are many,

You can walk on one, or combine any,

Everything is vibration and energy,

Purify with Yog, and flow in Bhakti!

Avi was perplexed and mystified at the same time due to yesterday events. He understood about meditation and its importance in growth but apart from that, what was all happening? What was this world he was entering? Was he ready? All these attacks, black magic, darkness!! He had thought meditation is all about healing, light and love. He was still to come out of Malvika's hidden dark secrets but what happened with Gauri shook his core. It was too much for him to process when he already had so much on his platter. All he wanted was to get out of this depression phase, may be find true love again and his soul mission to least. But this! It was as if some fantasy movie is going on. Battles between light and dark. No No! This is not what he asked for. He trusted Gauri and Tanmay but he had so many unanswered questions. Next day as they met, he was bit anxious and stressed out. Gauri sensed that; she suggested an outing to a Shiva temple, 'Shri Dudheshwarnath Mahadev Math Temple'. They went there, it was in Ghaziabad. The history of Shri Dudheshwarnath Mahadev Math Temple is linked to the Ravana period. It is a swayambhu temple. Shri Dudheshwarnath Mahadev Math Temple is very ancient and historical.

"What is this temple?" Avi asked, he had already started to calm down a bit as they entered the temple.

Gauri informed him "This temple is full of a different spiritual energy where your mind is filled with inner happiness as you enter. It is more than 5000 years old and believed to be since Treta yuga, much before even Shri Ram was born. This place has been the land of meditation and Tap for many Sages and Mahants. Lord shiva granted boon to Kubera's father Maharishi Pulastya because of his heavy penance. He also granted Kailash like place to dwell here that's why, Kaila village is near Shri Dudheshwar Nath Mahadev Jyotirlinga, short for Kailash. The Harnandi (Hindon) mentioned in the Puranas still flows nearby. It is said that the devotee on whom he is very happy, Lord Dudheshwar, blesses him or her with gold in abundance. It is said to be hometown of Sage Vishweshrava, father of Ravana. Both did ardent tap here and were gifted, Lanka of gold, by worshiping Dudheshwa, as per folklores."

Tanmay further added "If we talk about gold, I have heard it's because the shivlinga here has connect to Hiranayagarbha (the cosmic golden egg), that is why, the samadhis of the siddha-saints of the temple are located near to the 'Garbh Griha' (Sanctum Sanctorum). Many of these siddha-saints have taken samadhi, alive. It is believed that many miracles happen by worshiping these samadhis regularly. It is said that from the first Shri Mahant Veni Giri Ji to the thirteenth Shri Mahant Shiv Giri Ji Maharaj, everyone was a master in the art of making gold. Among the siddha saints of Shri Dudheshwarnath Mahadev Math, the name of

Tapo Murti Baba Elaichi Giri Ji Maharaj comes at the top. No one had ever seen Baba Elaichi Giri ji going out of the temple. Baba always sat near the 'Dhuni' and chanted the name of the Lord. It is said that many used to sit on the seat near the 'Dhuni' continuously for several days. This was his style of penance. During this period, he did not eat or drink anything or talk to anyone. When a person used to come to him with a problem, after listening to the sufferer, he used to say only, that he would tell Lord Dudheshwar that he would save you, and then used to shut his eyes and started muttering something as if talking to someone, within."

"Wow! That is so amazing guys," Avi was both excited and perplexed while roaming the temple premises and feeling the energies over there.

After darshan as they sat on bench outside, Gauri asked Avi,

"What kind of energies are you feeling here?"

"I am feeling very calm and at peaceful, something is mystical here. It is like I can tap into the energies of all those sages and saints. Can you feel my voice, it has also become so calm. I never thought any temple would do this to me. Since childhood only I avoided going to temples with my parents. It always used to be so boring, may be because of the programming, like go, bow down, worship, ask for any wish, take parshad and come out. But today, I don't know, I feel so different, and I feel it is not about the temple more but about me opening to various things, my perception changing, programming being decluttered. When you were telling me about its story, I could feel and see all those sages meditating and smiling at me and like a smile came on to my face automatically. Am I going crazy? Or is it all my figment of imagination as I am reading stuff on spirituality, the talks am having with you people. Is it taking a toll on me, or it is all real manifestations?" Avi asked as he patted his own head.

"Hahaha, no you silly. Because of meditation and awareness, you are rising above those sheep herd rituals, we keep following and doing without even asking why and what for. Mostly, going to temples, worshipping, is either based out of fear of higher power like if I don't pray something bad can happen to me or like for some deals, say a barter exchange; God, please grant me this and I will give you 1kg Ladoos. And if not these, then just because our parents tell us so or sometimes just out of curiosity, like tourists, we pay a temple or a sacred place a visit. We never try to feel deeply or live the story behind any temple or any sacred place for that matter. But when we try to feel the energy there and become one with it, if we can, you know, sometimes our consciousness can rise to another level" replied Gauri.

"I agree, because even logically if we see, some temples are very mystical, because of the collective high positive vibrations over there that have accumulated since yonks, just only if we can tune and listen to it. We can know the story of every temple or any religious structure for that matter, without even reading about it, we can, unfold many deep secrets that no one can ever tell you. Of course, though this tuning gets more refined as our senses heightened with purification of blocks inside us by sadhna. You remember Gauri how once in Almora we decoded mysteries about Kasar Devi Temple just by closing our eyes and feeling. You know Avi, we just randomly saw that place and went to visit the temple. But man, there was a tornado of energy there, so we decided to meditate there and like the whole story about that temple revolved in front of our eyes like a movie. Then we confirmed about the story on google and our minds were blown away because it matched to what we saw. After that whenever we go to any sacred place we always try to feel, tune, and live the vibrations over there" Tanmay gushed like a kid.

"Yeah, I remember! Can never forget that experience at Kasar devi. It was such mind boggling. So, Avi let me now ask you something. So as the story goes about this temple, Ravana also worshipped here and was an ardent devotee of lord shiva. He is not considered to be an idol human, in fact, a demon king and that is how Ramayana came into being, victory of good over evil or light over darkness. But tell me one thing, if Ravana, would not have been there, would Lord Rama be Lord Rama? He would have been an ordinary man otherwise. It was him, Ravana, who subtly pushed Lord Rama to battle him to show world how light and love can overcome any darkness. So, we can either judge Ravana the demonic darkness or we can change our perspective to see him as the great worshipper of Lord Shiva, a priest, who just played his role as a medium to push Shree Ram and let whole humanity learn a huge lesson".

"True! I never thought like this Gauri. I guess it is all about perception, but still why darkness must be there at first place?"

"Do you see this fallen leaf from this tree?" asked Gauri.

"Yes Gauri, seems like it has withered away" he said.

"Yes Avi, but why do you think it has withered away?" she asked calmly.

"So that new leaves are born".

"What if never ever any leaves fall and die. What will happen?" again she asked?

"Well then it will be forest earth and not human beings earth" he chuckled.

"Bingo Avi, it is a nature's cycle, life and death, similarly darkness and light. The earth will become overcrowded not to forget there will be other problems too. There are beings who are herbivorous, some are carnivorous, and some are omni. Now who is right and who is not? A deer being an herbivorous is right or a tiger who eats the same herbivorous deer, and is a carnivorous, is right?" she asked.

"Yes Gauri but still.."

"Wait Avi, let me complete" she cut him off.

Tanmay added "hear her patiently dude, before her own fierce form comes out".

"Haha Tanmay, very funny, now listen" she said.

"The temple we just visited you saw a picture depicting his different forms in a painting above. One is Lord Shiva, the Adiyogi, but he also has a fierce form of Mahakal the destroyer just like shakti is a divine compassionate mother but also fierce Mahakali that slays demons. Can we judge any of their form? And why do you think what was the need of such fierce forms? When it is all love and light?"

Avi shuddered, Gauri knew what he was thinking and doubting about.

She further continued, "When we start growing, we start getting aware of other forces as well, but it also happens vice versa. But does it mean we get afraid, fearful and step back from our journey? Understand the core of it. This whole universe was created with two forces dark and light. Have you ever thought why dark holes, vortexes, supernovas exist along with life giving planets? If there will be no night, how will you see the bright stars or what value will they have?

Usually brightest of stars shine in darkest of nights. These dark beings, spirits are like our challengers, they challenge us, push us so that we can know where we stand and where we have to work upon. Like last night I came to know I am not as strong as I thought and still have so much more to learn, especially my subtle fears which I didn't know about, but thanks to them, now I know. It is all about how we perceive and see full picture. To get blinded by fears and unawareness and then giving up is very easy Avi, like, very easy. But to understand why it happened, how we reacted to such situations and how we can work upon ourselves accordingly is the real deal".

"You are right Gauri, so right, I am sorry, I got scared a bit" Avi was bit repentant.

"It is okay, it happens, when we are a novice on this journey, new on this path and we do not know about various forces, our mind plays a little here and there. That is the reason it is suggested for newbies to always make a shield of divine light and then meditate, although they exist around us and it is natural, it's just as we start getting aware about them, so does they. Normally people cannot feel or see them because their senses are closed but doesn't mean they are not there. Though there is no reason to be afraid or scared, their path is different, that is it," said Gauri,

"But why are they like that, these dark forces, asuras, demons and even humans who become dark and adopt various ways to hurt others. What do they get? We don't say anything to them, we are simply growing, following our journey then why?" he wondered.

Tanmay tried to explain this "Every soul has its own place under the umbrella of cosmos. Its own role to play, its own dance and its own tune. The darker spirits also are the part and ansh of parmatma only. If creation is important, destruction is equally important. If light beings are important, darker ones are equally critical. But there can never be a perfect one side, neither total light nor total dark, and it should never be. But yes, there can be an order, where both can co-exist. And whenever this order gets broken, avatars come, or the other side comes into action to restore the balance. Presently, the darkness is increasing, and light is not. The main reason behind it is the loss of trust in humans, ego including subtle ego, greed, insecurities, getting materialistic pleasures through money, power, position; losing connect with the divine, imbibing tamsic gunas, no focus on righteous things, falling prey to the rat race, society bondages and all the shackles of the world, no self-love, blah blah, and therefore the light workers, like us, and many more on this earth, need to raise our energies, create a conscious awakening, raise the energy of this planet collectively, so that this order remains under control and earth can transit smoothly to the next yuga."

Gauri further acknowledged it "Have you ever wondered why some humans or spirits (since there is not much difference between them, just human have one extra layer of clothing called body) choose path of darkness or hurting others? Mainly if we can understand the pattern of them even like criminals, it is mainly because they were somehow devoid of love, compassion, understanding in some part of their journey. Me and Tanmay, have seen so many such spirts and when we give them love some of them transform to light beings. But yes, some, who have already chosen this path whether humans like some hard-core criminals and demons, then that is their choice. Why to judge them, who are we to judge them? Judging them is very easy but we as aware souls, can we try to understand what made them the way they are? No one chooses to be evil. If we cannot understand the real reason of that, then at least we should not judge them and leave it all to laws and cycle of karmas".

"You mean to say it's okay to be like that to hurt others, kill, etc".

"No Avi I never said like that, if we judge anyone, we create a block inside us too, because we let our egoic mind overtake, oh we are superior to them, which is also called superiority complex. No one is perfect Avi, all the spirits were created with permutation and combination of three virtues as we have discussed before. Just intensity varies in different individuals and how much we are aware enough to know what is right for our journey, which virtue to feed and which to tame. For example, anger is something we all have, some admit while some justify it and some feed it so much that it converts to rage and revenge. Like an ordinary man sometimes experience outburst of anger on family, friends but regrets it later and tries to control it, a murderer feeds anger so much that in some extreme circumstances they give onto it and converts it into actual action, while an aware being, as soon as anger starts bubbling inside, they come to know and tries to control it even before it comes into reaction. While enlightened saints have completely evolved anger to understanding and compassion for other souls and is free of this pattern of action and reactions. So, you see this tamsic virtue is in all, just percentage can be less or more. So, what right does it gives to any person to judge the criminal, when he himself is not completely devoid of those emotions or feelings? An enlightened soul will never judge and will try to understand the core of this anger in that person, like may be childhood exploitation or trauma, followed by lack of love and support in his or her life. Law will do its work but why do we have to fall down in our ego driven consciousness by judging any person or being in this universe. Remember outer darkness is just a tool or medium to push us to face our own inner darkness and transform them eventually. We can actually try to be grateful to it to be honest. I hope this explains better".

"Yes Gauri, it was an eye opener knowledge and perception, I never ever thought this way. We were, you know, always taught about either right or wrong, black, or white, I never thought this journey is all about being a panda. Amalgam of both dark and light in a balance. Sometimes greys are also okay, nothing is never totally right or totally wrong. It is all about our perception and understanding".

"Yes, and so is this journey. Outer forces and all sometimes help us to show mirror like challengers, do you know what is the real deal? Facing our own inner demons or tamsic virtues and transforming them" said Tanmay.

"Yes, this is Kaliyuga, more than outside it's more about inner battle" added Gauri.

"I think I am getting the zest of it, suddenly after having this conversation a guidance envisioned me, you both confirm about it. You said we all have both light and dark self, just like Lord Shiva and Shakti have and many other divine beings. I suddenly remembered once Tara saw a vision in trance state a form of me like some Greek god wearing white silver dress, once I myself had vision when I went to Pashupati nath ji temple of some tiger self of mine. Is it possible they are mine higher light and dark selves?" He was suddenly flustered.

"Wait let us see and feel about it and confirm from Lord shiva" Gauri and Tanmay closed their eyes in dhyana.

"Yes Avi, I got a strong feel, and a nod, they are indeed your light and dark self. I saw a faint glimpse of a light figure with silver golden light like a monk or saint, handsome like a Greek god and a man with tiger like face and human body very ferocious but ardent worshipper of Lord Pashupati Nath Ji. You will get their names and more about them as you will become aware, their stories and how it impacted your spirit nature and human births" Gauri replied.

"Wow yes it makes sense, that is how I envisioned it. Though how does that make me as me or defines me?"

"These higher selves are not somewhere outside only in some other dimension but also inside us, as part of our spirit. Perhaps, the hopelessly romantic as well as universal love you feel, the compassion, sensitivity, empathy is your light, yang which you have to balance with your yin or dark self which embarks taking stands, being ferocious enough to draw limitations to not let yourself drained for others, help weak ones, basically using power to grow and help" Tanmay showered wisdom.

"But there has to be balance in both, like if you imbalance light you will be drained, consumed, controlled by others because of over compassion and over empathy, with less self love and care, so the yin side balances it off by helping you to draw boundaries. Similarly, if yang side imbalances it may offload you with too much aggressive power, ego, completely neutral and angry from world and your own self sometimes manifestation of guilts and insecurities as well. So now you know why balance of both is too important. Once you start merging with them as your chakras will awaken more and kundalini activation happens you will be able to channel and become of them more." Gauri said.

"Understood now Mr Handsome tiger" Tanmay chuckled.

"Well, many girls have complimented me about the handsome part, so now I understand why. Jokes apart I am understanding it now guys. Most of that fear is gone", and his phone rang, it was video call from his home.

"What to do of this control and possessiveness, sometimes parents are scarier than any dark beings" he laughed as he showed them his call.

They all chuckled while walking back for lunch.

"Guys, I'm thinking of planning a trip. What do you say?" asked Gauri.

"But what about your work and office?" asked Avi.

"It's okay. Some salary will be deducted, but who cares? We won't take back a single penny from above, so let's not be robots and take a break for ourselves too," she said. "But are you both up for it?" she asked again.

"Count me in. A trip with you guys, I can't miss it," said Tanmay with a smile.

"With us guys or with Gauri?" Avi teased Tanmay in a mumbling tone. "I would love to, Gauri, but I've got these calls from my family. They're pestering me to come back," he said.

"Why? Are you a kid?" Tanmay teased.

"Nowadays, even kids are freer," Avi sulked.

"Then it's time to tell them you're not a 13-year-old and stop treating you like one," Tanmay said loudly.

"Don't even get me started there. They've been doing daily video calls asking where I am, what I'm doing. It's emotional manipulation," he said with a despairing tone.

"Gosh, dude! My parents stopped doing that eon ago. What's their deal?" Tanmay asked.

"Control and possessiveness," said Gauri, "We humans are conditioned in weird ways and practice possessive and controlling behaviours in the name of 'love, care etc'. Love is all about setting the one you love free and do you know soul's basic core is to be free. That is why most of the people now a days feel suffocated in relationships because parents, spouses think we raised him or her, married, now we own them. So put handcuffs around them and follow them or control them. It is sometimes sad to see it. Love, which is such a pious feeling, has been reduced to a joke" she said downheartedly. "And the worst part is that even some souls which have potential to transform, to awaken, to grow, to evolve, are under these traps and false love which they feel in the shape of care, affection and doing stuff for people like making food, making clothes for them, buying things for them. They think by doing this they are doing their share. And the other person since not buying things like them, not making food for them or stuff like that, does not love them enough and they only know what love is. Is it a barter exchange? Why the love is not felt from heart and is measured in quantities, like I did this for you, did that for you, what you did? This is a 'false ego' which they consider to be love. And, by the way, where there is an ego, can there be love? Aren't these two opposites?"

"But I also feel it is not just their mistake but also of the one who let it happen to them. My mom tried this onto me when I started this journey, but I made a firm stand, and told her that "This is my life, my journey, and my heart say it is the right path, so I guess what you are doing here is your own emotional insecurities. The fear of losing me is forcing you to control me. Yours and mine journey can be different, as we are different individuals. It was your choice to bring me to this world and raise me but if it is not done unconditionally and with a condition that when I grow up you will bind me, it is not fair mom". I told her "If you love me then please trust me and your upbringing, set me free." Thank God my mom understood and slowly accepted my path.

"Yes Tanmay, it was her lesson too. And you really helped her there to learn what is unconditional love. Parents often misunderstand attachment with kids, as love, but what they think they are doing is caring for them, it is actually the reverse. Their ropes of attachments create obstacles in a kid's journey. Our journey is not becoming mirror image of them or creating a version of their dreams and aspirations. It is about finding the best version of our own self; our heart resonates to". Said Gauri

"You are right guys, you know what I do not care, bring it on! Tell me where we are travelling?"

"Rishikesh and Vrindavan" she twinkled.

"Wow okay, any connection between the two?" asked Tanmay.

"Well one is city of yog and one is of love" she smiled.

Tanmay murmured to Avi "God only knows what this girl thinks, and like how and why".

"Does even God know? I seriously doubt Man!", he winked.

"I know you both are talking behind my back" she shouted as they entered then nearby restaurant for lunch. "Can we have our lunch?" She said with curves on her eyebrows.

"Aye Aye Captain!", Both laughed.

Next morning, they all started for Rishikesh. They booked a self-drive cab and went ahead for the trip. The distance from Delhi to Rishikesh was for 5-6 hours approximately. The Road Map was set. Delhi-Meerut-Muzaffarnagar- Roorkee-Haridwar-Rishikesh. Breakfast at Bikano Food Court at

Muzaffarnagar and Lunch at Chotiwala, Rishikesh. Tanmay and Avi will drive in parts. They were chatting, having gala time together and thankfully the weather was too in their favour. They started talking about spiritual things and then came up with an idea to play a rapid fire round on spirituality. Gauri became the one to play or to answer the questions while Tanmay was the one who posed questions.

"What is Meditation or Yog to you Gauri?"

"When you are that much aware that you know what is happening inside & around and why!"

"And what is love?"

"When you can *feel* what is happening inside & around and *feeling it for each and every being unconditionally*"?

"What is Self-Love and how it culminates?"

"To fly free leaving every worry behind, to a place where there is all the love beaming out from you and gushing back in you. Where there is no difference in you and the surroundings. Where you become one with everyone & everything and everyone & everything becomes you. Where your heart flows as if the river of joy and love are spreading over the whole earth, whole universe, whole cosmos. Where you rise above from the form and go into a state, where you, the form, and formless has no difference. You don't need any human to experience love. Then, my dear, you have attained self-love."

'What are the two biggest blocks in the road of spirituality?"

"Attachment and Expectations" Gauri answered.

"Now can we stop this game and listen to some songs instead. You people are boring me!" Avi frowned.

They played their individual playlists. Tanmay played mantra music, Enigma, Karunesh music while Avi went for some nice sufi numbers and his favourite coke studio. Gauri tuned into classical music and beautiful bhakti songs, and all three of them were flowing, differently and for different persons or reasons though, but why does it matter anyway. A flow is a flow! And they were flowing!

They crossed halfway and their convo started again.

Avi asked Gauri, "You had said Rishikesh is about yog and Vrindavan about love, but we are on path of yog and meditation then why do we have to go to Vrindavan? I know about these paths too, once, Tara had told me about it. But we have already chosen this path of yog then what's the need of love?" He asked wondering.

"First of all, Avi, for god's sake, please tell us about Tara!! You have mentioned about her so many times now we can't control it, tell us about her." She literally pleaded.

"How about I talk about my love in city of love Vrindavan, as you said, what say?"

"Aaargghhh Avi!! So not fair" she softly hit his back.

"Everything is fair in love and war" he winked.

"Can we now talk about the paths then? I am intrigued too as I follow only meditation" Tanmay growled.

"Such a spoilsport you are", Avi snarled.

"Okay guys think about one thing before we start. Have you ever wondered about a plant which gets sunlight, water, air but no space and fertilizer. How will its growth be?"

"Ummm, may be vertical or less growth" Tanmay said.

"True. It may grow less or may grow just vertical but will not be like a full round grown up tree. Sometimes ambulation of various ingredients is the key to a full growth at all levels and not just vertical. Same is the case with the four paths, **Karma Yoga (Actions), Bhakti Yoga (Devotion), Rāja Yoga (Meditation) and Jñāna Yoga (Knowledge)**. If you ask my spiritual journey, each path had been very important for my growth. Without knowledge I could not know how to do yog, without yog I couldn't purify my inner koshas infused with blocks, without purification I cannot still my mind enough to feel divine love of my Isht. So, you see, it is all connected. If I talk about karmic path, I feel it is not just doing mundane activities or filling responsibilities but more of performing various tasks like spiritual ones, helping people, travelling to discover more etc. So, you both tell me how can following just one can make this journey complete?"

"Interesting! So, if any name can be given to this amalgamation of all paths what will it be?" Tanmay asked.

"YOGBHAKTI" Gauri replied. "Purify yourself through yog that is Gyan and Tap and then flow in love or bhakti for paramatma and ultimately merge which is devotion".

"Who is your Guru and Isht Gauri", Avi enquired.

"Mine, well you are heading towards there to meet my Guru and Isht", Gauri replied with a divine smile on her face.

"As in?"

"My Guru or Guide has been Shiva, guiding me through dreams, visions and sending various mediums in form of some spiritual people, books or divine gurus like Mahavtar Babaji, Lahiri Mahasaya ji, Saraswati Ji, Budhha Ji. Their teaching has been the core of meditation. I have followed kriya yog which has been dawned upon me by Shiva at times directly through him and other times, through Babaji or Lahiri Ji. And my Isht, is Shyam. That is why we are going to Vrindavan as well. When you will tell me about Tara there, I will tell you about my beloved as well".

"I understand about various paths and why all paths somehow are important for our growth, but Gauri we cannot go on all at once, how to know from which path to start first on this journey and then maybe then slowly attune to others however the need arises?" asked still jumbled Avi.

"That's quite a valid question. In fact, so many people are clueless from where to start and which path to follow. I would always suggest, first, see what your core is, like Tanmay's Pranamaya kosha is strong, or you can say has less blocks because of his past birth Sadhana and the prominent *ras* of his soul or divine self (it is formed at the time of soul creation), so his core is yog and that is how he started. Mine Manomaya kosha have less blocks along with my divine self ras of love, so my core is of devotion and that is how I started. It just came naturally, so we flowed and followed at least in basics of it very quickly, much practice was not needed there. Like Tanmay started with basic pranayama and I started with chanting of mantra of Shyam. That's like surface level cleansing of our koshas so that we can advance to next step accordingly. Some people also start with Gyan or knowledge as their Vijanamaya koshas have less blocks. But it doesn't mean other kosha blocks are not there, and that is the main lesson to remove them which can be done with other paths. It is not like if you stay on one path, growth will not occur, it will just it will take lot of time. But if we collect **pearls** from every path and start practicing it along with our core then the **dance to moksha** takes less time, with a smooth flow. Like to remove my lower chakras blocks and make my mind still, to balance between mind and heart, I chose meditation and to expand my higher mind I also studied lot of holy books. While Tanmay's main lesson is to unblock his higher chakras to feel oneness, pure love, whether for formless creator (Parabrahm) or form (Isht) and then eventually for entire cosmos. And to answer your next question, how we know about it, well I would say, be open, take at least one step towards it and help comes in various ways. For instance, our inner voice of soul gives signs in form of dreams, intuitions, while cosmos helps us through our guides (human or spiritual), signs, universal numbers, symbols etc. The key is to just walk with strong will power and surrender making sure to not get stuck out of conditionings and ego to one particular path. Real deal is not which path you follow but how much flexible and open we are while walking on it because so many times the sacred divinity we believe in send us help in various ways, but because of our shackles of ego and stubbornness, cannot see, feel or hear and that becomes ironical."

KOSHA
the 5 psychic sheaths

anandamaya kosha (bliss body)
vijnanamaya kosha (knowledge sheath)
manomaya kosha (mental sheath)
Pranamaya kosha (vital air sheath)
annamaya kosha (food sheath)

"Woah, okay I guess the picture is quite clear now, but you mentioned something about soul creation and all what is that?" ever eccentric Avi asked.

"Avi, my curious Einstein, you are not ready about that yet, or, if you want your brain to get fried !!' she chuckled.

"Better to zip my lip", Avi responded.

They reached Rishikesh well in time. It was already lunch time, so they made their way straight to 'Chotiwala Restaurant' near Ram Jhula and ordered Thali's for them. It is one of the best restaurants in the Rishikesh and quite an old one. After resting, near ganga banks for a while, they went to Bhootnath Temple. Very few people know about this temple as if it is intentionally hidden but Gauri had an insight to visit this temple in her dream. Bhootnath Temple is believed to be a place where Lord Shiva stopped to rest during his travel to marry Sati en-route to Daksha's place, the father of Sati. The deity is manifested here in shiva linga form. The temple has several floors and a deity's worship place at every floor. It has amazing and breath-taking views of the whole Rishikesh. In the middle floor of the temple, there is an open area where there are four bells around and a Sphatic Shivalinga (Crystalised form, which is self-made after the snow remain frozen in glaciers or mountains for like thousands of years and become hard stone due to compression). All three of them were feeling supernatural powers here. Something was different totally. Avi stood beneath a Bell there and asked Tanmay to stand in the other one, while Gauri was meditating in a nearby place. They rang the bell, and woah! It felt, as if the sounds of bell, cleared all the blocks in their chakras. The energy started flowing like properly throughout inside their bodies. And the trance they felt in their head was another level. It was as if some therapy session they had just taken. They went to

Gauri to tell her, who had by the time, opened her eyes after meditation. However, she was in a trance state too. Avi touched her shoulder to enquire if she was fine. She saw Avi and smiled.

"What happened Gauri? All well?"

"Yeah! The energies are so fine and pure here. As if the yin - yang energy or Ida - Pingla Nadi flow, strongly balanced here which led to flow of Sushumna Nadi leading to Shunya state almost like a samadhi." She could hardly speak more because of her intoxicated state.

"Ohh! Yeah! Me and Tanmay had similar experience beneath that bell", Avi told her everything they felt.

"One more thing but. I got some guidance or what, but just look at this place. It has so many floors, from bottom to top. I do not know, but it feels like to me that every floor connects to one chakra. But in its reverse image what we see normally. Like, the bottom hall, connects to the Crown Chakra, like connecting us to the divine. And the top of this temple, connects us to the Root Chakra, the centre of Shakti. Getting an extraordinarily strong feeling about this. And in between, the floors are connecting to the chakras in the middle. I guess these main floors are also eight in number. Like the seven main chakras and one Bindu chakra," said an enthusiastic Avi.

"Wow! That sounds cool! Finally, our boy has also started to feel the unseen and expand" Tanmay said.

"Hey! Why don't we go to each floor and feel the energies on our respective chakras. I have a strong feel each floor's respective chakra energy will balance our own chakras, what say?" Avi said with so much energy that it radiated in smiles of Gauri and Tanmay too.

"Let us go partner", Tanmay said and all three of them then went to each floor. They felt energies in abundance. It was such a beautiful spiritual experience for the three of them.

"Now I understand why this temple is hidden and not many people know about it" claimed Avi

"Why?" asked Tanmay.

"Well not everyone is ready to understand its mysticism".

"Very true, and now you know why I got this guidance from shiva to come here, this is how helps comes for what we need most at right time and we expand" she said with this feel of tranquillity.

Happily, merrily, they went out of the temple and spent their evening then at Parmarth's Ganga Arti. After such a beautiful spiritual experience, the Ganga Arti at Parmarth Ashram was another level. The Shiva statue in the Ganga, on the banks of Ashram, and those sacred lights, the chants, the Artis, it was so divine. They literally had tears in their eyes, as they could feel the love of Ganga Maa flowing towards them and like Shiva is blessing them with putting hands over their head. Shiva and Shakti both! Something was different in this trip. They were becoming more aware and as if some petals of wisdom were getting opened. Like they were unblocking some spiritual gifts, which were due. And may be that is why this trip to Rishikesh happened. Everything happens for a reason now Avi understood so well. They went on to their hotel. Had their dinner at hotel itself, played with each other and danced madly to some bhakti songs like Sufis do. They were experiencing time of their lives. Avi never thought in wildest of his dream, trip to a spiritual place is like not less than some serene adventure and what's best with his soul family, his people!

"Avi! One more spiritual task for you" Gauri Said.

"Now what? I am tired. My third eye chakra is revolving like crazy! As if I have taken 10 bottles down".

"Haha! Can understand. But see, in this state, you will be able to perform better my friend", Gauri said with a smile.

"Okay. What is it?"

"See my Aura!"

"Wait, what? How can I see your Aura?"

"Close your eyes. And see the colours around me. Try to look deep and what do you see, just tell me."

"Okay. Trying." I am seeing two colours; one is yellow and the other one is pink."

"Great!! See it more closely Avi. You are seeing it quite right but there must be one more colour. See it deeply and try to see if the yellow colour has another texture or something".

"Okay. Umm, am seeing white colour as well. Actually, I saw it previously also, but I thought it is like a trail or cloud on which the other colours are resting. Does white also counts as a colour?"

"Of Course, Yes. So, what is the sequence of these colours now? Like which colour is closest to my body and then so on"

"Well, first is white, quite a lot of it. Then Pink and then it is Yellow"

"Bingo! Thought it as it is!"

"And?"

"Well, our Aura colours depict the present state of ours, and not just the colours, but their thickness, texture everything talks basically about your present emotions, mental being, and state. Like you saw white as first colour. White means the colour of peace, calm, and tranquillity. This am feeling since I had meditation there at Bhootnath Temple. Now, next colour you saw is pink. Pink signifies love. Since I felt love of Ganga Maa and, since morning I am feeling Shyam around, am oozing lots of love for everyone. I am literally flowing in love at the moment, and it is beautiful. And yes, at Bhootnath Temple too, I felt the love of Shiva and Sati, which I forgot to tell you as I was in such a trance state. So overall, yes, so much love, and pink colour justifies and like confirms it well. Now let us come to the third colour. You saw it as yellow. It is not yellow, but golden. See, the newbies who start seeing Aura, sees golden as yellow, as golden is quite a refined colour and is not seen so easily. It takes time and growth to see golden, as golden."

"And what does golden signifies?" Avi asked.

"Golden means knowledge, wisdom. Since am reading a lot now a days and getting lots of guidance through Shiva on various things, you saw golden, or yellow as you said".

"That is cool!"

"But how to know whether I am seeing right or wrong?"

"Your heart will flow if you see it right, I mean that is how I know I am seeing correctly, and it is not mind's imagination or something. Heart flow is like a green flag. And am so happy that you could see Aura like this. Normally people take time, like months to even see one shade of Aura. But you were like bang on Man! Cool!"

"Hehe! May be due to that bell vibrations, my all chakras got opened" he chuckled.

"Ask Tanmay also to see, why just me? he rolled his eyes.

"I am seeing since childhood all these things, I am a pro in it," chirped Tanmay.

"Tanmay, tame down your boastful egoic "I"" sternly Gauri said.

"Sorry Guru Maa". Tanmay said realising his mistake.

"Now guys go to your rooms, let us sleep well. We have lots of things to do tomorrow as well. Good night, my wolf pack"

"Owwwwww!" Both made a wolf sound together and bid goodnight laughing all the way.

Next Morning, they went to Goa Beach after breakfast. Goa Beach is a small beach on the banks of River Ganga near Laxman Jhula. Due to its white sand, it resembles the beaches of goa and is often called by this name as such. It is a favourite spot for taking some dips and sunbathing. A lot of tourists come here for picnic. The area is very beautiful, the breeze coming from the ganga feels so cool on the face. The whole scenery there, the ganga river, the white sand, mountains, weather, it all makes it a place to be.

Gauri, Avi and Tanmay, spent some time there. Did meditation and had a long walk on the beach. The morning energies were pristine, drenching, and beautiful. From there, they went to the market of swargashram, close to laxman jhula & goa beach. They did a lot of shopping there, some yoga T Shirts, Yoga Mats, small accessories like tote bags, necklaces, and earrings, Rudraksha Malas, and some other souvenirs for their family and friends. Roaming in the market and shopping, made Avi remember the shopping with Tara in the Paltan Bazar, Dehradun. He saw a pair of peacocks in a shop. What came in his mind, GOD knows, but he just picked that pair of peacocks, perhaps, in the memory of Tara. Around noon time, they started their journey to Vrindavan, which was around 7 hours' drive from there. To reach Vrindavan, they had to come back to the road they had taken yesterday, as they had to bypass delhi anyways to reach Vrindavan.

Vrindavan is one of the prominent places of Braj Bhumi in Uttar Pradesh as Lord Krishna spent most of his childhood days there along with his divine consort Radha Ji. It is located in Mathura district and is the most sacred place for Krishna devotees. They were to visit two temples here mainly, Radha Vallabh Temple and Shri Banke Bihari Temple.

They reached Vrindavan till evening. Gauri went mad as they entered the outskirts of Vrindavan. Her inner child like came out and she was swaying. She had tears in her eyes, as if someone comes back to his or her abode after a long arduous journey. It was evident from her eyes that she belonged here. She pointed some white birds who were following their car like see, 'they are our divine angels. They are welcoming us here.'

This place did something to Gauri. That is why she was elevated like a kid for going to Vrindavan more than anything. On their way to temples, she was dancing and flowing on the roads of Vrindavan like Meera would have swayed in the name of Kanha. She started buying bangles and earrings like a teenage girl, like she wants to decorate herself for her Isht. She was singing songs, swaying, posing dance mudras, like hugging herself and flowing in love and bhakti combined. Everything around her like faded, she had no awareness all she could feel like a gopi in love for her lover. Avi was perplexed seeing her like that, the ever-composed Gauri! He never imagined this form of her or roop, even in his dreams. He was like asking his own self and wondering, when suddenly he heard the voice of his soul,

'Is there any difference between bhakti and love even? What is the difference between that of a love between Laila Majnun, Rumi Shams and Meera Ghanshyam or Krishna. Bhakti, Sufiyana or love, it all means or signifies flow. To just devote and surrender yourself totally to some person, Soul, or the Deity. It is like complete surrender, no conditions, no judgements, no opinions, nothing. Just dancing to the tune of love, or bhakti.'

They then reached their hotel which had a beautiful garden, Gauri ran towards there and asked Avi and Tanmay to do chikli with her. Seeing her love, her devotion, her madness, and now this chikli dance, suddenly Tara flashed before Avi's eyes, and he got emotional. Tears started rolling from his eyes. Tanmay tapped him from back, and he composed himself as they walked towards their room.

"What is this place Tanmay, I am feeling so overwhelmed and emotional form my heart. The vibe here is so different from Rishikesh. There it was like my blocks are going out, balance is coming, awareness is expanding getting purified, felt lot of serenity at spirit level while here, like ocean of love started to flow from heart and soul, like someone came and touched my soul. As if am at my real home Tanmay" Avi got sentimental.

"Aww, Gauri is right, your soul is very loving Avi, you yourself don't know." Tanmay was surprised seeing this state of Avi.

They took rest in hotel there and after dinner, as he had promised, he started telling them about Tara.

"How to even begin to tell you about Tara. The love of my life! The love, which I can still feel so vividly inside. I met Tara when I was posted at Dehradun. There was a short trip to Mussorie and Chakrata by a trip planner, and I along with one of my friends there had gone to this trip. It was three days trip and there only I met her, and slowly we came close, and by the time the trip ended, we became love of each other's life from complete strangers. At times, the length of time spent together doesn't matter much, but the quality of time spent in those moments, matters the most. Those two-three days were the most beautiful days of my life. How on earth I don't remember any other moment so vividly as much as I can feel and remember those moments which I shared with her. The love, between us, was so pure, so unconditional, so divine, it just can't be described in words. She is not just beautiful from outside; she is indeed much beautiful inside. Her soul like, so compassionate and sentimental, but still like shakti maa, so determined as well. In a moment, she would act like a kid, cry making stupid faces in acting, and in just another moment, she would start showing her intellectual side and will give you wisdom like no one can. Such a sweetheart she is. I loved pulling her cheeks in market of Paltan Bazar. And she was like, stay away you idiot, I don't like this PDA. Hehe! Such a fun it was with her. I was completely lost, or rather, I found myself completely with her, around her. She made me feel complete! As if perfectly fitting in to my life. I can still remember her breath on my chest. That feel, I could feel never again. With every breather, I was like getting more and more content. As if nothing else just matters. Like my soul was getting nourished at that moment. She made me feel love as love!

The way, she used to see me, like a breeze coming from her side and waving me throughout. Her gazes were so intense, so deep, can't even describe. Her moist eyes, seeing me, I can lose anything for that. I can die million deaths to be with her. Even if I have to buy a single second to spend with her, I am willing to do anything. She loved playing chikli, that game where we hold our hands and dance or jump. I never did that before in my life, due to you know that reserved kind of a nature of mine. But with her, it was so pure love, that I could not even think of anyone around me but her. Everything as if did not exist. Everything and everyone zoned out. It's just she and me.

My hands still can feel the warmth of her face. I can still feel that kiss I made on her eyes, those drenched and emotional but happy eyes. I was a chain smoker Gauri, yes, I was. She had once asked me that why I smoke. I had no answer, but she knew, that I used it for suppression. She had asked me to reduce it, rather leave it if it is possible. I had told her that day that I would try to reduce. And see, I quit it. I don't smoke anymore. I had tried so many times earlier as well, used those nicotine-based chewing gums as well, but could never do. Don't know why and how, I wanted to do it for her. Though I could quit it this year itself, especially after I started meditation, but still. It was all for her. Can do anything for her! Just anything."

Avi fell silent for some time in her memories. Gauri patted her back and Avi started again.

"Have You seen the leaves of a Tree?

How they dance to the tune of air passing by,

That leaf is me, and that passing air is Tara!

Have you seen a star up in the sky, twinkling in the moonlight?

How that moonlight makes it shine even brighter,

That star is me, and that moonlight is Tara!

Have you ever heard the music coming out from a Sitaar?

How when the fingers meet those strings and such a sweet music exudes,

That music is me, and that Sitaar is Tara!

Have you seen any painting on a canvas?

How some strokes of colour from a brush, makes wonders, and create a lively portrait,

That canvas is me, and those colours is Tara!"

Gauri had tears in her eyes listening to all this. She remembered her own flow with her Isht, Shyam.

"She had given me this pendant Gauri. I still carry it with me all the time. The other half is with her."

"She had some lucid dream or vision that night, that we need to walk on our paths alone for some time. She had used some words like soul partners for us and had said that we are meant to be together but not now. For her that night was like serendipity, with a promise of beautiful tomorrow, a tomorrow, which never came again.", Avi fell silent with a husk in his voice.

"It was all lonely without her. A part of me was gone forever. I so miss her. After she went away, I met a lot of girls, you know, for marriage and all, but could never connect with anyone. The purpose of life as if was lost totally. For months I could not sleep properly. Every night I used to scroll her photos on my laptop, my mobile. The nights used to be like, am lying on bed, watching the ceiling, and doing nothing. Literally, nothing Gauri! At times tears would fall, but there would be no trace of sleep. I used to go numb! It was just her memories. It took me like yonks to stand again. Then came Malvika and you know what and how I got married to her, now. But one thing this marriage made me understand Gauri. And that is, that what does pure love means! What does that flow means! The flow, the love, which I could never feel with Malvika because it was always expecting, controlling, possessing from her side. The care and all were considered love and not the true virtues of it. Tara's love, I could never feel with her, and I know, I can never feel it again. I was all down and drowned in all this when you came Gauri! And slowly, steadily, I am getting better. I still miss that love but atleast that one ingredient which was missing in my life, the self-love, is bouncing back, little by little. And I understand now that when my own reservoir is not full, how would I be able to give water to others. When I, myself lack love, self-love, how I would be able to spread it to others. Thank you so much Gauri, Tanmay, for your support and love, unconditionally in this journey. Had you people not been there, I don't know what I would have done with my life. I don't know what is there for me and Tara, in this life. Whether she will come back to my life or not. But one thing is for sure, I love her from my core. Wherever she is, whatever she is doing, I feel my love can reach to her.

I have been in love before too, but this, I just can not feel it again. At times it feels so empty inside, like I just want to leave everything and run into her arms and lie there. Just lie there, like a kid. Her hands caressing my hairs. So, want to feel that warmth again. Where are you, Tara? Come to me! Be my friend, if not partner, if the society or your family bounds you not to be. I will be happy if you will just be around. Come in any relation with me, but just be there please! I don't need any label on our relationship. Just come as friend if not more. But just come to me. I will be happy just seeing you around. Will make you happy when you are sad. Will hold your hands when you need it. Will give you a hug when there will be things putting you down. Will do stupidest things to make you smile. Will play chikli with you. Will listen to all your blabber and yeah, you blabber a lot, but I want to hear it all. I will never get bored of your talks. I will never get tired seeing you. I cannot live without you; you know that don't you? Oh, Divine beings! This vast universe, the whole cosmos. Please!! Make her come back to me. Please!", And Avi started sobbing.

"Aww!" Gauri gave Avi a hug with tears in her eyes. She just could not leave Avi as if a mother consoling a sobbing child. After a while both were fine and smiled at each other. Who was thanking whom, was a true mystery.

"Soul partners, the soul mates or the twin flames she must be referring to" Gauri said.

"So, what is the difference between karmic, soul partners or mates and twin flames?" Avi asked after settling a little.

"Suppose the soul "A" had an experience with Soul "B" and there is some left over from the birth 1. The same shall be carried to subsequent birth(s), be it birth 2 or any subsequent birth, till the times it gets negated completely. If we do not square up the same in time, it continues to subsequent birth or births. This creates a "Bandhan" a circular bond where we keep coming (Travelling) with these souls over different births to settle these actions but due to our blockages, closed visions which happens over the time due to our experiences, we don't get it done. Until and unless this baggage gets empty, the soul enters an un-ending round of births and re births. And at a point of time when soul reaches that maturity and squares up all the bad actions with good actions, the soul gets free from earthly/ worldly attachments and 'bandhans' and gets ready for her final travel to the place where she was created or any other place, higher or lower to her creation place, based on her actions. These actions are known as "Karmas". Since the soulmates are few, we mostly experience things with Karmic partners. These lessons, over the different births makes us learn things and grow. With Malvika, you seem to have a similar karmic relation while with Tara either soul mate or even twin flame."

"What is Twin Flame?", Avi asked.

"A twin flame is a purer form of a relationship. With lots of definitions and meanings around on the internet, basically we can say, that it is one soul, living in two bodies, like half in each. They are the mirror to each other, with deepest understanding, influence over each other as well as deepest disagreements. They can heal each other like anything, they can understand each other like anything, but since they are a same soul, they can have fights or separations too frequently than they have with others. They reveal your true self, if your good things, then even your darkest virtues.

Twin flames are getting united more now a days than ever as the consciousness is rising. Mostly, in recent twin flame revelations, it has been observed, that while one of the twin flames is aware, has raised consciousness, the other is largely blocked or drowned or struggling. This awakened one, then helps the other half to rise or awaken, and then they both raise themselves individually as well together and spread spirituality together. They serve humanity together, through travels, through healings like shamans do, writing about spirituality to create awareness or through some spiritual centre, creating some other sect of spirituality as per their visions, and other alike things, and spread happiness, love, compassion, spirituality to the mankind. This relationship is just not for themselves but for the mankind at large. When these two ascend, they create this world a better place. They need not be husband and wife necessarily, but their love, their connect, their bond, their unison is at the deepest level possible as they experience that love, which drenches only the soul. It is almost like a divine union. Their energies create magic when they meet in real. With Tara, I assume you have a twin flame relation or a soul mate, this, now you need to find out my friend."

"Okay. Getting it. Thanks man and Gauri. Can understand a lot of things now. Thank you, guys, like so much. By the way who are your twin flames Gauri and Tanmay?" Avi was curious to know about them too.

"I am still finding mine, I thought I found her but... let's see" his voice had bit of disappointment which Avi understood.

"Mine as I told you is Shyam" Gauri was smiling.

"But he is a God, isn't he?" Avi was startled.

"Well, my divine self is a Gopi so yes, it's possible. The love I feel from him, even at spirit level, cannot match any human love I have felt till now. I cannot even express it. No words can describe that feeling" her voice was trembling. Avi and Tanmay never saw her like this, the calm composed Gauri suddenly filled with so many emotions of *virah* and love at same time.

"You are talking like Jogan, like Meera, do you miss his physical presence you know someone you can touch, hug at human level" Avi asked.

"I do sometimes Avi, I won't deny. At the end I am experiencing this human life with a gift to feel all the emotions. This virah sometimes is so strong to see him and meet him for real. Then I close my eyes and feel him in my heart, near to me, in me, around me and Avi it then feels like he was never ever far. His soul and mine soul are right now dancing to tunes of his flute in the blue world. That world is not just up there somewhere but also inside me.

Space, distance, physical presence is all just maya induced illusions, but the reality is true pure love is never dependent upon any of this. If you are awakened enough to let that divine love flow into you, he appears to be so nearby. You know once I cried in viyog, he said I was never far from you my dear, it's you who couldn't see me because of your mind created walls and curtains. I always have been here waiting for you when you will look at me and come near to me. Not only a devotee is dying to be with his Isht but also the Isht, please come to me soon my dear. Awaken and purify your consciousness that you go deeper into anandamaya kosha where your soul is and that's where you will find me waiting for you. Feeling his love and merging in him is my moksha" she said almost bursting in tears.

This time it was Avi and Tanmay's turn to console her.

She further continued "Shyam has been a constant source of love to me. Whenever I felt down in my life, he has, in some way or the other, never let me feel love less in my life. Actually, because of his presence around, as well as, inside me, I never wanted any human's love in my life. That is one of the reasons I never had any relationship in my life as I never had this emptiness inside. That is also one of the reasons I don't have many friends or connections for the simple reason, that I can channel this divine love anytime inside my heart, which drenches my soul like splash of water cleaning and purifying everything."

Next day in morning they went first to Banke Bihari temple. Bankey Bihari, originally named as 'Kunj Bihari' is believed to be a merged form of Radha Ji and Krishna Ji. As per legends, the temple was established by Swami Haridas who was guru of famous singer Tansen and is considered 'Lalita Sakhi' from Dwapar Yug. Swami Haridasji had, on the request of his followers, had sung a song in praise of Radha

Krishna or Shyama Shyam. On seeing his devotion, Shyama Shyam had given him and the followers darshan (appearance). Swami Haridasji requested them to give him dasrshan in their merged form and that is how, kunj Bihari or Banke Bihari idol appeared in Nidhi Van, which was later moved to Banke Bihari temple. It is believed to be the original idol or statue of that time. Lalita Sakhi is the prime sakhi's (Friends) or gopi's of Radha Ji. Normally the temple remains hugely crowded and it is very difficult to have proper darshan. But somehow, they were able to have darshan so beautifully. It is said that the devotee is incomplete without his deity and the deity is incomplete without his devotees. As much as devotee wants to have 'darshan' of his prabhu his Isht, similarly, the deity wants to see and feel that pure devotion of his true devotee. Gauri had tears in her eyes throughout. She also had mentioned that she was a gopi herself in Dwapar yug. Maybe she was flowing in that love and must be in some leela. Avi and Tanmay knew they have a bigger task on their shoulders today. Not making arrangements for the trip but to handle Gauri who was going crazy here in Vrindavan, Brij Bhumi, her abode.

As they entered Radha Vallabh temple, that is nearby Banke Bihari temple, they made darshan and sat there for a while. Radha Vallabh Temple is beautifully made, and the energy are so pious there, that any true devotee is sure to lose himself there in flow of love. It is believed that the idol of Radha Vallabh ji is not man made but it was given to a devotee by Lord Shiva himself, after seeing his devotion. Gauri was swaying like anything in this temple. She was completely lost like as if her divine self merged into her. And Avi, could not help himself but to see her with moist eyes. Suddenly Avi had tears in his eyes, as he was looking at Gauri who was like just physically here but rest somewhere else at all levels.

"Avi? Is everything alright?" Tanmay asked.

"What happened Avi" Gauri opened her eyes suddenly after hearing it all.

"I am feeling a very pure love coming from your soul to mine. I have felt this before as well but never said anything. What happened?"

"I am good Gauri, but I am feeling so much overwhelmed with these sudden burst of emotions" his voice was cracking.

"What emotions Avi" she asked out of concern.

"What all happened with you, our discussions, this trip, that day when you had come and touched my soul through healing something like opened in my heart, some layer. You did something to me which my soul knows Gauri."

'Aww Avi yes, I saw your soul as in your divine self and hugged it. I was overflowing with so much love like a mother feels for her kid I couldn't stop myself. I feel I have this gift to touch souls of people".

"Of course, you do, because your core is of love and devotion, your heart is so pure Gauri," said an emotional Avi.

"What happened Avi, I feel like you want to share something. Do not hesitate, tell me kiddo".

"Gauri! I have a penultimate devotion and surrender for you. I really do not know why and how. But I so want to like, you know, keep listening to you, like a devotee listens to his "Isht" or deity. I at times go numb in front of you like what I should say, such kind of emotions keep bursting inside my heart which I never felt for anyone. I see you and feel I should offer you something like flowers or something and make you sit on some raised platform, not at all next to me, as you cannot seat next to me but somewhere up. Not saying I feel this all the time, but whenever I feel this, I feel it so strongly. To Press your feet, to do your "Seva", like a true devotee do, whatever you say without a question asked. To make you sit in some swing, like the one where Lord Vishnu ji is lying on the serpent 'Sheshnag' and keep you swaying in that swing with my hands slowly slowly so that you can sleep peacefully in the ultimate bliss, like Maata Yashoda did with Kanha Ji. No one disturbs you then. Do little little things for you, and like stop or turn all the discomforts, any, from your way. I have seen you many times sitting on an elevated platform where you are giving wisdom and knowledge to people, and I am making all the arrangements. That place so looks like somewhere in this Brij Bhumi, may be Vrindavan. A big land, where you are teaching spirituality and I am like the main caretaker there. Just listening to you the whole time and flowing in so many emotions. I have felt tears trickling down while you are making the speech. Have also felt you as some goddess, some 'Devi", whom I am doing complete seva like making you ornate with jewels, decorating you with flowers and other natural fragrances, making daily arrangements, your bath, clothes, prayers, your food, your minutest thing which you need and what not. As if to do that is one of the biggest purpose of my life", Avi said it and started crying.

"Aww Avi! Come here, let me hug you. That was the sweetest thing that anybody could have said to me. Iam so proud that I got such a devotee, Hehe. We all are equals Avi, no one is up, and no one is down. But I acknowledge your sweet gesture. It is so overwhelming that my heart is flowing like anything for you at the moment. May GOD bless you with choicest of blessings. And you must have tap into my Gopi form. I guess you are one of my Sakhi or sahchari", Gauri said and ended with a chuckle.

"It really gives me bliss Gauri to feel that for you and I would love to be your sakhi or sakha or sahchari, whatever", Avi said with an eloquent smile.

"Come. Let us eat chaat and lassi outside. It is in that gali of Bank Bihari ji. It is mouth luscious. And Tanmay you being a foodie are surely going to make the shop keeper's fortune today as you will not be able to stop yourself for sure".

"I don't eat that much!"

"Yeah Yeah"

Next, they went to Nidhivan. It is the most prominent places of Radha Krishna as it is believed that Radha Krishna along with their gopis, sakhi's, still performs the 'Rasleela' here in the night. No body is allowed, as such, to stay in night there. It is a forest of tulsi (basel) trees, and it is commonly believed that these plants are Gopi's or Sakhi's only, and they transform themselves in the nighttime for Rasleela. Every Tulsi plant is found in pair here, signifying Shyama Shyam or Radha Krishna. Gauri was too emotional here. She was running in the premises as if she knew the place already. She had tears along with the most divine smile any person can ever have. It felt to Avi and Tanmay, as if he merged with her Gopi form totally today. Avi started humming a song as Gauri started to dance there, "मैं प्रेम दीवानी हु, तू प्रेम दीवाना है".[4]

They were happy for Gauri, their Sakhi.

They went back to Delhi and then to their respective places. It was an emotional time for three of them. They were feeling and talking like how good it would be if they can live their life like this together. Where there is no judgement, no opinions, lots of fun and banter, there is always one person

---

[4] A spiritual song sung by Gopis for Lord Krishna

taking care of others, where there is so much understanding between them. Tears were not stopping even if they tried it so hard. But they had to move on for their places.

Avi was working on himself with more concentrated efforts now, after having these discussions, this trip and what happened with Mr. Purple and all. Three of them were back to their towns again. He started to take stands a bit, started reading more, started to have spiritual discussions with colleagues, travelling to some places he used to get visions of, feel the energy of those places which used to give him a boost or an ascension to his growth. Tanmay and Gauri too were working on their spiritual journey. The power and strength within were at another level. They used to even meditate together through online meetings and had been doing a lot of spiritual tasks together, as they got visions from time to time. Along with their own journey they Helped wandering spirits to pass over, healed and read people in distress physically, emotionally or mentally, spread divine knowledge and awareness. The trio also sometimes spread love to entire cosmos by channelling divine love and hence were becoming more and more integral part in raising the collective consciousness of Earth, but little did they know it was just first step in their spiritual journey.

Chapter 10

The Tunnel

Believe in the plan the cosmos has send,

Leaving you, for yourself, to fend,

Have the grace & strength to walk this tunnel my friend,

You shall find 'yourself' on the other end!

Upon returning home from their trip, Avi encountered a storm of challenges. The turbulence from his previous journey, where he dared to defy his family, had lingering effects. At times, he stood his ground, and other times he kept his anger and frustration in check. But the constant barrage of emotionally charged taunts and sarcastic comments from those around him left Avi withdrawing and speaking less.

His wife, Malvika, was also becoming increasingly insecure, adding to the already high levels of tension and resistance in their home. Her insecurities and need for control only made Avi's situation worse, as he found himself distancing himself more and more from her. The angrier she got, the more he pulled away, creating a vicious cycle that left both of them struggling to find a way out.

Energy is an interesting game. When we go extremely insecure, angry, sad, or use cuss words or curse, we emit a very negative or if the feelings are too strong, even dark energies. And these energies hit, to the people who are attached to you. And when there is too much high energy at one end, and too much negative or dark energy on the other, a strong resistance appears. He was surrounded by resistance and darkness at home itself. Some days he used to be fine by beaming high energy from meditation, but some days completely drowned as these negative and dark energies from his family, used to suck it. As per Fourier's Law, Energy moves from high to low. This exact used to happen with him. His high energies used to work as healing energies, or strength for others. It is like suppose a bird, full of flesh and bones, gets stuck in the vultures. What would happen? In minutes there will be no flesh and bone, forget about even bird. Similarly, the low energies suck the high energies, as the energy flows from high to low through threads of attachments or fear or illusion of being separate souls. Once these shackles are overcome nothing and no one can affect even one percent because we start to manifest everything as one. But Avi still had to go long way to understand and become it.

Avi was feeling the weight of the family's emotional manipulations. He was constantly questioning why they couldn't understand and accept his path. Although Gauri and Tanmay were his friends, he felt a deeper connection with them, where he could be himself and experience pure love. However, facing his family every day was becoming a struggle, filled with bitterness and low energy. Despite meditating, he felt trapped by these obstacles, like a fish caught between water and land, longing for her true home.

Avi realized that his attachments, fears, and lack of self-love were holding him back. It was his choice to choose the path he wanted to follow and have the willpower, determination, and fearlessness to pursue it. Once he made that step, the universe would open countless doors to help him. The ropes of attachment to Malvika were also making him vulnerable to spiritual attacks, fueled by her anger. Avi experienced headaches and fever often, but as his senses awakened, he was able to self-heal or seek help from Gauri or Tanmay. However, he was becoming too reliant on them.

"Avi please focus on working on your weaknesses and ropes. These relationships and all keep changing every birth, they are like co passengers on train so there is no reason for this much attachment. No family member or friend or anyone is your ultimate destiny, to give them so much energy that they start controlling you and you start getting affected so much. It is your journey. When you travel in a train do you get attached to your passengers? You only talk, interact, laugh, enjoy, share emotions, and slowly they all get down at their respective stations. We came alone, and we will die alone. This is an individual journey! So do not give anyone this much power that they start feeding on you. The relationships we make here, on earth, are just to teach us many lessons and drive us to growth, that is their purpose, but we attach so strong threads with them and forget the real thing. You are growing now, and your frequency is rising, there will be many patterns, labels you won't connect anymore, and you must let it all go. If you don't do it on time, a resistance will start coming in you, a tiff between your soul and spirit. While soul pushing you to set your path right, let go of attachments threads while sprit still tied to those because of weaknesses. This may cause dark night of soul pushing you to state of void. The soul, spirit and body must be in harmony. It is a huge misunderstanding if you let go of attachments, we let go of relationships or have to leave our family. It is basically rapturing your own created golden cage of mind, for which we have the key, but we don't want to open. We are afraid to fly high in sky, we do not understand the love that flows without any attachments, threads, labels, is the real pure love. That is the main lesson our spirits have to learn and that is why we keep incarnating in this cycle. In each birth we become so much attached to present family members due to Mayic illusion that we forget they keep changing like clothes every birth. Your mother may have been your daughter or friends in some other, your some far away friend would had been your spouse in some, so what is the point to attach to someone that is not even real or is temporary.", Tanmay used to make him understand this hard lesson.

Avi grappled with the tension between his own path and his family's expectations. Despite his struggles, he was slowly cutting the ties that bound him to their emotional manipulations, but his fears and sensitivity held him back. His family frequently accused him of being selfish for following his own path, but he saw them as opportunities to learn and grow. He was making progress in other aspects of his spiritual journey, but he still struggled to break free from his fear and attachment to his family.

He began withdrawing from them, limiting his interactions, and retreating into his own space. He felt like a traveler caught between two boats, unable to fully choose his path. But he knew he needed to decide soon, before he felt completely suffocated. On a particularly difficult day, he reached out to his friend Gauri for support.

"Gauri, I know you have been helping a lot and guiding but action and choices I have to take only, but no matter how hard I am trying, doing meditation, I am just not able to cut threads with my family or letting go off attachments. Actually, I don't want to hurt anyone in this journey and quietly keep growing, but I do get affected when they are not able to understand me and keep coming under Malvika's spell. Due to this, not only I am facing so much resistance at my home but also inside me. Please help me, I do want to choose the right course and overcome these ropes, but I am not able to" disappointed he was.

"Calm down, I understand your position. We all have different flaws to work upon. You said you don't want to hurt anyone; but are you ready to keep getting hurt in the process? This pattern has been continuing since your childhood, supressing your own emotions so that anyone else don't suffer. You know what the problem is with being so over empathetic, in pretext of not hurting anyone, eventually hurt themselves and drown in this sea of suffering. They give so much and are not able to comprehend where to draw lines for healing their own selves as well. You think you are saving them by bearing it all but what you are doing is feeding their ego more and more on cost of ripping yourself completely. Plus, it is not going to help them as well."

"Help them?" he was confused.

"Avi, if you choose them to learn lessons about control, insecurity, and mental barriers, they also chose you to show them the light. By cutting your attachments and fears with them, they will gradually understand what they are losing and the negative impact of their egoic behavior. This realization can bring about positive change for them. By not taking this step, you not only hinder your own growth but also rob them of the chance to grow and evolve. The journey may be difficult with moments of anger and discomfort, but the end result can be a beautiful journey of self-discovery and growth."

"I'm trying my best," Avi retorted. "I can feel myself growing, but this is something I just can't seem to do."

"You might not be trying hard enough or not at a fast enough pace. Remember, if you can't love yourself, you can't love others or help them. It all starts with self-love."

"I don't know Gauri. I am trying is what all I know at present." He sounded lost.

"Okay let us do one thing. Let's try the spirit journey to spirit world if that helps" she suggested.

"What's that !?" he questioned.

"In order to understand deeply the reasons of some circumstances or our shackles, when the time is right this experience of spirit journey plays an important role. What we did earlier was to a past life on earth to know about a particular block, but this will be to another dimension or world where we go after our deaths, as spirits in between carnations. That world is called spirit world and it vibrates at much higher frequency than Earth."

"You mean there exists a world that is not on earth but in some other galaxy or dimension?" he was so curious with this completely new revelation. He had heard about aliens and all but this !

"Yes Avi. As per Hindu Vedic philosophy, you must have heard about 14 lokas or worlds (7 above earth and 7 below). Some also call it as other dimensional spheres starting from 4D-12D. The first Loka or dimension above earth, for simplicity, we may call it as 'Ancestral world'. That is the reason that many people reveal, who have had NDE (near death experiences), that they were greeted by their loved ones at the end of tunnel. Here many spirits kind of heal, rest, analyse the past births with the help of guides, before going to next human birth on earth or other life enduring planets. In dimensions more far above the ancestral world, there exists demigods, many higher selves of aware souls, light beings, the elders or sapt (7) rishis, the trinity etc. These worlds are not visible through naked eyes or technology because it vibrates at much higher frequency. It can be envisioned though through meditation as Ajna or third eye chakra open or through trance hypnosis. The latter is now practiced in many countries but it has limitations to access mostly and they go only till spirit resting world in fourth dimension which is very near to Earth unless the soul is already gifted to access much more" Gauri explained.

"Yes, I have heard about it, but why do you feel I need to take this session and by which method will we do it?" he was puzzled.

"Well, many times people on outside may appear to be normal functioning but there are so many deep-seated provocations of blocks and distress that are masked from any medical personnel, psychologist or even our own selves. The deep-seated fears in you that are not letting you cut the threads of attachments to be free no matter how hard you are trying. As you started to meditate, these blocks were pushed to come on surface of which before you never knew existed because they had become part of your Vritti (spirit nature). Now the next step is to find a solution how to let go of this by going to that related past birth and then spirit world, to see the complete picture. When we visit individual births, we only see chapters of particular block respectively but in spirit world like we see the entire book and the pattern of our spirit nature. We also meet our soul family and guides who have been helping us all along. The mind and body our spirit preoccupy, is this human form, and is obstructed and polluted by so many past lives karmic seeds and captivities, illusions. But above, there, our remaining spirit is much purer as it is our higher selves. The method that we will follow will be traditional method as you have been meditating so your first door of Ajna chakra is opened, I will also channel and open more of it, so that you can smoothly transit". She explained.

"What do you mean by remaining spirit" his mind was completely boggled.

"We are never born with full spirit energy on earth in human body, as our brain have limitations. According to our lessons, we come normally in from 5%-50% of spirit energy in human body. Remaining part stays in upper world, also called pure higher self. As we awaken, we start to merge with it, expanding our consciousness, channelling gifts, and enhancing at every level. Saints, Sages, Avatars etc, who are liberated souls, are exceptions, and only come to help humanity have more than 50% of spirit energy in human body, that is why their intelligence, wisdom and miracles are at par since childhood. So, in this session the recovered spiritual memories will also bring new insights, meaning and comprehension to your life as we will analyse from both perspective, human element and soul element. In spirit world you may also meet your family higher selves living and deceased, your guides, gurus etc who may give and show the purpose of this birth, your mission, and the core reason of your blocks." She tried her best to make him understand this complex concept.

"Will I see Tara's higher self too?" suddenly his heart raced.

"Perhaps! Depends on what is needed to be shown to you. I can only take you to this journey, rest your guides will take over. Remember, *they will show you what is needed, and not, what you want!*"

"I understand. You feel I am ready for it?" He doubted a little.

"Yes, you are, as you have meditated enough to open first door of your chakras. So, in this session, conscious mind interference based on conditionings will be less. Moreover, you know and have accepted your blocks, and are struggling and desperate to grow and get over this pattern and cycle now strongly. Else I wouldn't have suggested this to you if I felt you are not ready" she smiled.

"Cool. So, when are we doing it?" he asked excitedly.

"Well, for this we will have to meet. It may not be completed in one go, may take 2-3 days depending upon many factors. I have a spiritual task ahead in Devprayyag (Rishikesh), Tanmay will also join me there, you can also come there" she suggested.

"Okay, I will get leaves from office but again my family will make ruckus" he suddenly sulked.

"Avi, at one hand you want to follow your soul mission and on the other hand you cannot even get over such petty fears. It saddens me to see this as I see so much spark and potential for you to grow. It is not a coincidence that we all met at this point of life! You take one step forward, but the flaws push you back two steps. At any rate, start loving yourself this much to get hold on your free will and choices. It is not like that you are going for drinking, partying, or drugs. Your heart knows that this is the golden chance to finally set you free, even then can't you take stand for it? We should follow our heart, our soul, when we are sure that it will bring new happenings, new opportunities, new growth avenues and the best part, closer to ourselves but still, we at times, due to society or family control, chose the otherwise. Are we humans or robots?" Gauri felt a bit anguished.

"You are right. My heart says first time in my life, I am doing something, that matters, is and will be meaningful, will give me contentment, pure joy, and bliss. Now, if I can't take simple stands on this, then what will I ever do in my life. I will do this! Tell me when and where to come?" he felt strong bold power awakening from within. It was like, if not now, then probably never!

Tanmay was supposed to join the next day for task. Gauri and Avi reached a day before for the spirit journey session.

They first went to Rishikesh and took a cab from there to reach their hotel at Dev Prayag. Dev Prayag is one of the "Panch Prayag's" of Uttarakhand, that is, five sacred confluences. It is the place where Bhagirathi and Alaknanda merge and River Ganges flow. The union is a sight to behold. It feels like a magical reunion of love creating the most sacred and holy river, Mother Ganges. The place also has an ancient temple which is dedicated to Lord Rama.

After they took rest, next day they started with it. Their hotel was like a camp near banks of Alaknanda. Gauri told him to lie down and relax, releasing all the tensions in body and mind. She further explained him "After pranic breathing, opening of chakras, I will take you to deep trance, and in the moments of your last birth's death. From there your spirit will fly up above to the passage to the spirit dimension"

"So, are you ready?"

"Yes" he was bit nervous but sound of serene flow of Alaknanda visible from their resort calmed him down.

She led him into a deep trance and brought him to his final moments of life as a freedom fighter in the Punjab province around 1878. "What do you see?" she asked.

"I see myself being shot and my spirit leaving my body and floating upwards, like a cloud, towards a golden gate. It's a relief to be free from that life of anxiety, aggression, and violence," Avi said. "As I approach the golden gate, I see a shadow in silvery blue light slowly coming towards me. I feel emotional and it's like someone is giving me a warm blanket. I think I know him... It's Yedi, my guide," Avi said, with tears in his eyes.

"Yedi hugged me, and it was like healing for my battered spirit that had suffered so much violence," Avi choked out.

"Go on Avi, what does he do next?" she whispered softly.

"He is first taking me to a chamber... trying to figure out what is it...it's like a healing room... where there is like a shower of loving and soothing energies with hues of white, baby pink. As I step in there, I feel so much lighter and very much healed from my last birth scars. It is like the dirt is shedding from my body and am getting lighter... Wow!! I am feeling so relaxed.... Next, I see an open grass field, and a white castle, there I see so many souls... there is someone coming close to me...I feel I know it...this energy... it's a female... ahh okay she is my current birth mom, I recognise, she is from same spirit group. She has been incarnating with me in many lives to help me learn an important lesson, which is, how to love myself and take stands. And I have been helping her how to love unconditionally without control and possessiveness. My dad seems to be from other soul families like in group of new souls, I can't see that for now. His classroom is like different from mine. Yedi says soon I will leave this spirit group after this current birth as I am growing nicely and will transcend to a higher class or dimension. He is happy with my current progress; he says finally your choice for this difficult birth have started to show its colours. I am asking him where have you been when I had been in so much pain in this life time. He says well who's voice you heard on the beach in Mumbai when you had thoughts to drown yourself... the sudden boost you felt after that... universal numbers and symbols you kept seeing in your life... 111...555... I always was there my boy... these are the signs we give.. if only you can understand .." Avi was shocked beyond belief. He took a minute or two to compose himself.

"Do you see Malvika?" she enquired.

"No" after a while he replied.

"Ask Yedi"

"Yedi revealed that Malvika's higher self was trapped in a dimension not of this world due to her current choices on a darker path."

Yedi then took Avi to a library where the records of past lives of spirits were kept. After human deaths, spirits came to the library to study and understand what they could have done differently to improve future lives. Yedi helped Avi examine his own akashic records to understand his core problems. In previous lives, Avi had repeatedly separated from Tara or let her die young due to insecurities. This had deeply ingrained a fear of losing those close to him, leading to self-doubt, guilt, and an inability to love himself. These blocks clouded Avi's judgement and decisions. Gauri whispered, "Ask Yedi for solutions."

After a long pause Avi continued, "He is taking me to this void.... It is like a tunnel but with very light matrix. ...Hues of diamond blue, feels like not every spirit can float away in this because of its light framework of frequencies...... Okay! I see this world, another dimension perhaps from before.... There are mud huts all around, trees and group of saints (seers).... They all like wearing saffron attire and doing sadhna of... I hear Shiva... the whole place is like that of some grand ashram with no boundaries... There is so much serenity, love, calmness flowing in each atom that's here...

The collective consciousness here is like chanting and dancing in similar rhythm of divinity…… Yedi is taking me to a particular hut where I see a seer smiling at me… I feel I know him… my spirit has been here ages ago… His Aura and glow is nothing like I ever seen before … It is almost blinding my eyes. He is toning down a bit, looked in my eyes and saying… Welcome my child." Avi got silent as tears silently rolled down his cheeks.

Gauri gave him a moment or so and then further asked "Who is he"?
"He is my Spiritual Guru under whom I have trained eons ago as my higher self….. I feel before this human incarnations started …His name is Rishi Markandeya, and I am his disciple…" he said gently.

"Oh great! Ask him for his advice" Gauri was as much surprised as Avi, she always knew he is gifted, different and have strong connect with Shiva and Kanha now she knew why.

"Yedi is one of 'gan' or disciple of Lord Shiva. His role right now is to guide incarnating spirits in spirit world. They all are Shiva devotees, so am I, that is why my connect with Pashupati Nath Ji (one of his forms). Rishi Markandeya says, you are doing well my child, but you really have to start working on the ropes one by one if you have to really get over this loop of birth and death… It starts with forgiving your own self first because of the mistakes you made in your past lives and lost your loved ones…. It is okay, we all make mistakes, it is all a dance of illusions and learnings why to take it that seriously? What will you gain if you remain drown in it, sulking in it, will it help you? It is like a spider web where more you try to detangle it; more you will get tangled…… Let go of your fears! When you were here eons ago, even then you had this subtle fear that you will forget us as you start incarnating on earth.... You will be all alone.. from us...your soul family... Well, here you are, did anyone forget anyone?..... It is all an illusion... The love and connect we share is never lost; it is there, always.... It may change forms, but it is there.... Love lost in one form come around in other forms or mediums... but we get too attached to one particular form that when we lose it, we feel whole world has shattered and close ourselves to other mediums of love that choose to help us.... child don't feed you fear so much that it actually pushes you away in real, from your soul connects.... Where there is fear and attachments, does pure love can ever flow? In order to learn this lesson, yours and Tara spirit chose this separation so that you don't stick into same pattern of many births.... You chose Malvika in order to square off some past karmas and learn very important lesson what not is love in order to understand what love is and how to value it.... And that starts with loving and knowing your own self..... If you would have got everything on platter, would you be what you are right now? Everything happens for a reason! If you don't do in this birth, when you have so much help, you will have to again take birth with same family members, may be with different roles......it won't matter much here... time does not flow the same way as it flows at earth ... What is like one hundred years on earth is hardly ten days here.... We are waiting for you child... so is your Isht, Lord Shiva... So choice is yours Avi! ..." Avi just flowed in trance state...

"If you want to ask something from him, go ahead" Gauri guided him further.

"Why has my life been like this, Guruji? I lost my love in college, couldn't propose to her, then Tara left me. My marriage was filled with insecurity and control, manipulations, and games. Why have I been so unlucky in love when all I've ever wanted is love? Why has my destiny been written this way? I see so many people finding their soulmates even when they're not aware. What have I done wrong? Am I so bad that I can't even have the one thing I want in my life? I would trade anything for love, but I have everything but love. Why, Guruji? Why? Who wrote my destiny?" Avi wept, feeling helpless.

"You did," Rishi replied with a smile and half-closed eyes. "And are you sure you don't have love around you?"

He suddenly felt quiet, Gauri and Tanmay, how can he forget them.. he is right if I lost love so many times, I have gained also just mediums were different, but does it matter !! but he is choosing this current timeline of too much heartbreaks and separation so he asked again. "Me? No ways! Why would I write and choose such pathetic story for my own self? This much I have learnt in this current spiritual journey that there is an important reason and lessons for me but still why I had to be so harsh on my own self " he still couldn't comprehend this.

"Ahh, you have forgotten the choice of this present timeline you made before taking birth.. You have forgotten the white dome where you analysed deeply and with Yedi help made this choice of your parents, heartbreaks and spouse. You chose this life, and everyone has been a medium to help you in their own ways. Love can be transformed my child! It never remains the same. If someone is not loving purely does not mean that he or she cannot love purely! May be he or she have their own shackles.. stop your mind playing this victim thing… At the end, everyone is a soul having a bodily experience on earth. It starts with accepting others as they are, their own spirit dance… and the circumstances around you…. but without getting affected which can only happen once you let go of the attachments and that is the biggest lesson you have to learn in this current birth, and for you to learn this strongly you chose it... trust your higher self's choices, as it is wiser and more aware than human mind, surrender my child to it.. and then your future timeline will start changing as it is still an unknown blank canvas... what kind of painting will be created at the end of this birth will depend upon the colours you will choose now... Black grey or rainbow colours" Rishi Markandeya explained with a smile.

"Do you want to meet someone?" Asked Rishi Markandeya with a smile and takes him along. Suddenly he is transferred to a twilight sky, and he sees a woman... No a goddess.. wearing white drapes with stunning diamond jewellery. She is glowing like a diamond with so luminous light yet so soothing and pacifying. She is smiling at him.

"Feel her who is she" asked rishi Markandeya.

"She is.... That feel...that energy resembles so much like "Gauri" he started to shake.

"What?" even Gauri was shocked.

"Yes Gauri, I am seeing your higher self-form, you are a goddess illuminating so much love and compassion. She is now coming close to me and showing me a vision in the night sky of cosmos".

"What is it?" asked Gauri.

"It's like a rail track, a silver road, with multiple loops that lead to a gate where I see my spirit standing. The loops represent my past lives, and the present door is my current life. I see myself opening the door and stepping onto the track with ropes attached to my back and shoulders, slowing my progress. Ahead, I see beams of light in the form of knowledge, understanding, and healing from Tanmay, Yedi,

Rishi Markandeya. Beyond that, there's a dark tunnel with no one in sight. She says I have all the help and knowledge I need, but now it's time to choose and find myself. It will be a ***dark night of the soul***, but if I cross it without succumbing to negative emotions, I'll meet her and maybe even Tara at the end of the tunnel. Most importantly, I'll meet a better version of myself. But if I fail, I may not meet anyone because of the frequency difference. It all depends on my thoughts and feelings. And if I don't make it, I'll have to start again in my next life. She explained that it's all a dance, from creation to union, connecting with other souls, learning, evolving, feeling, and loving. Ultimately, it's a dance towards moksha, the ultimate reality. Some get stuck in suffering because they take the dance, song, and steps too seriously, but those who understand it's just a divine play, awaken and enlighten." Avi took time to process it all.

"Come Avi, it is time to meet someone else too!" higher self of Gauri whispered in that dimension.

"Who?"

"See yourself!"

Suddenly he is transported to a grassland… with greenery all around… midnight sky… grass and flowers are like pearls shining in the moonlight… Wait !! he has heard or seen this before… Tara she had seen this and told him in Mussoorie…Suddenly… He sees a swing hanging on a tree where a girl is sitting…. He can't see clearly… he goes near to her.. his heart in physical body started to race a bit.. he knew whom he is about to meet… As he approached her…

Tears starts rolling down from Avi's eyes.

"Tara!"

"Yes, Avi it's me... I have been waiting for this moment....Come, sit with me!" Avi gasped for breath of air even in his spirit form. Tara's higher self was so much more beautiful, pure, enchanting, glowing in a baby pink golden Aura... that it made him completely mesmerised... his human form had tears in his eyes again...

"Where were you, Tara? I missed you so much...!" Avi was very emotional...he wanted to just be here ...he didn't want to go back to his human self..

She caressed his cheeks and said with softest of voice "We had too many lessons to learn Avi, you have seen and felt it already, right? I had my lessons, you had yours. I am glad, that you have come this far. I knew you will! And time has come, when after this last step, we shall meet again, in human form too. Just this last step Avi. Just one last night alone, the dark night of your soul! Do this sweetheart. I know you can!" she also was bit emotional.

"I am tired Tara, my spirit is tired now... please come to me...I beg you,... meet me soon Tara.." he literally pleaded on his knees.

"Choose me, Avi. By choosing me, you choose yourself, for we are one, not separate," Tara said with a warm smile.

"But where is my higher self, the left-over spirit energy?" Avi asked, suddenly confused.

"Your higher self-travels between the higher dimension and your human state, depending on how turbulent your life is. It sends love and healing energy and guides you, but it also sometimes stays dormant. My human self-started the journey before yours and has merged more with my higher self. Yours will too, if you choose to merge more in meditation. Sometimes, during deep meditation, your higher self transcends and glows with me. Come soon, Avi, in all ways."

Avi started shivering, his body started turning blue.

"Okay Avi, now you have to come back in this body very slowly, grounded and open your eyes" Gauri said.

Avi took a while to process and comprehend it all... he was spell bound and emotional. So was Gauri.

"I guess it is all clear now Avi?"

"Will you leave me too Gauri?" He asked teary eyed, he suddenly busted out as he had an intuition after this session.

"Avi... nothing is ever lost; I will be there waiting for you. Now cheer up see the bright side you may meet Tara too, plus it is not like I am leaving you tomorrow" and they retired after an exhausting day.

Next day as Tanmay also joined them, they went to sangam. On their way, Avi described him about the spirit session with great zeal.

"Woah, Rishi Markandeya your Guru and Gauri a goddess, I am feeling so small in front of you both great personalities" he teased.

Gauri asked them what kind of energies do you feel here in Devprayag?

"It's different from Rishikesh that's for sure, like Rishikesh have bit mixed energies, neutral and calm lord Shiva vibe but here it is different kind of serene warm loving energy as if his higher heart chakra is resonating with ours own" Tanmay said excitedly.

"Yes, very true, this Sangam is not an ordinary one. It is a portal since Sat Yuga, a passage towards some higher heavenly dimension, like a passage. That time it was a coalition of all three rivers Alakananada, Bhagirathi and

Saraswati, if we can co relate it is like representation of Ida, Pingla and Sushumuna nadi"

"Wait a minute! Saraswati? Where does she come from? Isn't it a confluence of Alaknanda and Bhagirathi alone?" Avi asked mystified.

"I had a vision, I kept to myself. It's an ancient portal in Sangam, visible only to those who look with their third eye and feel with their heart. Created by the gods, it was a blessing for awakened souls to pass to the divine world upon death. Those souls who managed to balance the Ida, Pingla and awakened the kundalini shakti through sushumuna knew about this portal that went straight to a divine world like a shortcut which else would had taken many more births to go there. But as time passed and each age grew darker, the pure Saraswati was lost and the portal door closed. There's a long queue of spirits waiting to access the portal. Our mission is to help them pass over by channeling the divine consciousness of the holy rivers and assisting with our divine selves."

"Divine, not higher?" Avi asked.

"Yes, our godly selves, now don't ask right now about it, it is not time yet. First merge your higher self" Gauri said calmly.

"Alright still it is super interesting, I am feeling so blissed to be part of this, in a way if we can help directly or indirectly" an enthusiastic Avi said.

"Tanmay, you channel Bhagirathi pure energy, Avi you Alaknanda and I will channel Saraswati, then together we will direct to open it. Are you guys ready?"

"Aaye Aaye captain" they both said enthusiastically.

As they sat near Sangam, three of them closed their eyes ready to channel what was needed. Suddenly Avi and

Tanmay heard a shriek from Gauri. She was half in water holding to nearby chains and struggling to climb up, but the flow was too strong. Immediately Tanmay sprang into action and pulled Gauri up. Avi was too shocked to even react, as he came into senses, he saw Tanmay pacifying Gauri down as gave her his jacket to her as she was completely wet with cold water.

"What just happened?" he was trembling with fear.

"I don't know, I was deeply lost in trance when I felt suddenly someone pushed me into the river. But there was no person around us. I guess it was a very powerful spiritual deadly attack!" she was still alarmed.

"Oh my God, but how come!?" Avi went numb.

"Let us talk about it later and take ger first to hotel, as she may catch fever. Temperature is too low with strong winds". Tanmay was very worried for her,

Both of them took her to hotel, Gauri was still shocked, she could have died that day!

After few hours as they tried to recover from this incident, they attempted to figure what happened.

"What was it?" Asked Avi.

"It was a spiritual attack on her", Tanmay responded still bit anxious.

"What? How and who?" Avi was scared and tensed.

"The dark forces! And that includes the energies from Malvika too!" Tanmay replied sharply.

"What? But how she can?" Avi just couldn't believe what he heard.

"She cannot touch Gauri, but she can certainly touch you, you, being attached to her. And since, Gauri formed an attachment with you, so if not directly, the attack was done indirectly, with you being the medium or puppet here" Tanmay replied bit coldly and continued "Avi it is time for you to now walk alone in this tunnel, See, not just it will affect you, but also your loved ones like me and Gauri plus many more reasons you found in your spirit journey. Now you know why this tunnel walk is so important for you. It might take time, days, weeks, months or even years. But I hope you are mature enough now to understand and accept this, else it can put even our lives in danger, especially Gauri on stakes!"

"Don't blame yourself Avi, it's my fault too for getting so attached to you. The light will shine the brightest after this storm." Gauri felt sorry for Avi, knowing he would take it to heart and feel guilty. Avi broke down in tears. "It'll be so lonely without you and Tanmay, especially you, Gauri. How will I cope if you're not there? You know my situation with my family and friends, and with Malvika, I'm already becoming detached from everyone. I don't have any friends besides you two. If you and Tanmay aren't there, how will I survive this hardship? You've been my mentor, guide, and best friend. This loneliness is already overwhelming and without you it will only get worse," Avi said, overwhelmed by emotion. He didn't know how to let go of the only people he talked to in his life now.

"Yes Avi, I know, it will be very lonely. That is the way it should be. You are passing through dark night of the soul. Everybody has, everybody does. So, it has to be like this only. But, because of this solitude you will understand the value of self-worth, self-love. Maximum time we spend is with our own selves and if we can't do that, there is a serious problem. Normally what we do is, that we look for happiness in external events and get habitual, dependant and attached to it, so when it is not there we suffer. The real Joy, it is, within us, we need to find and embrace it and then shine it outwardly. But we choose to go the other way. We make outside happenings the main source of pleasure when it should be vice versa. You got too much dependant on me to fill that void but my boy it's only you who can, and this journey will help you detach and understand this deeply. We cannot be your clutch but just mediums to help and guide which we did. Think about it all and all the experiences you had with us and in spirit world. Along with working on your shackles do something you love as well like travelling and see world through new founded vision and perceptions. This will boost your growth inside out. Meet new people, share, make full use of your healing and compassionate powers. The compassion is your gift, Avi. The way you feel love as love, compassion for everyone, without any judgement or opinion or condition for a return love or compassion, very few people can do so. This period will make you channel this and make it your strength and not weakness. Remember, the gifts, can if make us strong, can also make us drown or weak. The same fire which cooks food for us has the potential of burning everything. So, learn to balance it and you will be able to manifest properly. You will feel contentment at another level which you could never feel till now. And always remember Avi, it is all inside us and I will be there with you, whenever you need me just close your eyes and you will be able to hear and see me" Gauri choked a bit. This feeling she was experiencing was very similar to like a mother who taught her son and now had to leave him in a hostel for next phase of his life. so, she had to be strong.

Seeing Gauri's state Tanmay tried to console Avi more "See it as metamorphosis. Like how an egg becomes a larva. Then from larvae to pupa and then finally transforms into a beautiful butterfly. But was it that beautiful colourful butterfly from start? No! The process of becoming a butterfly was painful, full of challenges, there was always a danger outside of being killed, eaten and what not, but after all that, how beautiful it becomes at the end after passing through all of those tests. This is your metamorphosis! Or see an aero plane. How, when it takes off, it goes through a turbulence. It faces all the atmospheric pressure but keeps flying with all that turbulence. After a while, the turbulence starts diminishing and the plane finds a balance. What was a turbulence just some time before, becomes a normalcy and it just not affect the plane anymore. And the plane can then fly for many hours just like that. This is nothing but that turbulent period because of the atmospheric pressure. Feel the pressure heads on and a beautiful flight awaits you"!

"But I will break in this journey. What if I won't be able to walk? Please be with me. Don't leave me lonely here" said crying Avi, no matter how hard he was trying he was not able to accept it,

"You have to walk this phase alone, dear! Everyone walks this phase alone. We are not leaving you or going anywhere, just walk through this tunnel and you will find us again. You can find it alone only. You cannot find it with the help of someone else. Some paths we need to walk alone. Find your wings Avi, find your 'own' wings like that butterfly. Everyone's wings are different as every soul is different, so is the journey. But first, find your wings and let us then fly together. This cosmos is waiting for us Avi and we cannot stop. We need to do a lot of things at large for the mankind, and we cannot do it with shackles, else disturbances come like at sangam today. Though we had a challenging experience but channel the energy in your third eye and heart chakra and see. How those aware souls who got pass over are blessing us from up above in the sky. Many more tasks like these are awaiting us! Many more spirits are waiting us, dead or alive, to help them in their spiritual journey. We can be mediums to many! And we cannot fly if we have bondages in our legs attached or we are in a cage. To fly, we have to cut the shackles, break the cages, and fly free. This tunnel will break those shackles. But since it is your cage, your own bondages, your own ropes, you only have to break free. Have you heard that old Chinese proverb, 'If you give a man a fish, you feed him for a day. If you teach a man to fish, you feed him for a lifetime'. This is time for you to learn how to fish, on your own. Go out, explore the sea, it is full of fishes, you just have to learn how to catch one for you!" Gauri was trying to motivate him the best she could.

Avi looked above to Gauri, who was sitting on a nearby bed draped in a comforter getting warmth and very tactfully hiding her tears and heavy heart.

"Time for us to go back and sleep, it was a very tiring day" Tanmay said, breaking the silence. They all went to sleep, but who could sleep peacefully that night was difficult to say.

The next day, Tanmay, Gauri, and Avi made their way to Dehradun, where they would catch their respective flights. Tanmay was the first to go, and before he left, he hugged Avi tightly and whispered in his ear, "Go find some girls on this journey." Avi forced a smile to hide his emotions. Then it was time for Gauri to leave. She hugged Avi and whispered, "I'm waiting for you, Avi. I know you'll come back to me and Tara after this journey. Goodbye, and loads of love!" Avi was speechless, still processing everything that had happened so quickly.

At Jolly Grant Airport, Avi wandered around, bought some cookies, and sat in a deserted corner. He sat there, lost in thoughts, until he fell asleep. In his vision, he was walking in a desert, following a star in the sky. Despite being tired, hungry, and thirsty, he refused to give up. Eventually, he came across a cactus and sat next to it, declaring to the universe that he would not lose. Suddenly, the desert transformed into a beautiful grassland, the cactus became a tree, and Avi saw himself sitting on a swing next to Tara, wearing a black tuxedo.

He was awoken by the final boarding announcement for his flight.

His flight took off, and he saw outside from his window seat. It was all white & grey clouds and a blue sky. It was raining. He was seeing the sky, gazing deep when there happened a lightening. He kept staring there while his fellow passengers felt afraid of the continuous lightening now. He kept staring at the continuous lightening, and murmured, as if talking to that invisible power. "Take me to the tunnel!"

acknowledgements

(स्वांतः सुखाय, वयम सुखाय)

"Lord Shiva" and **"Lord Shyam"** for being constant inspiration, guides, mentors and what not. Even if I pour all my gratitude in words, it will not suffice. This book belongs to you, I being just a medium for writing it. Thank you for making me believe in the cosmic plan and to treat every soul as soul, beyond the realms of human body, inter alia. I am a novice, a learner, a seeker, who has just put steps on the pedestal. I wish this guidance, these insights and this love in abundance which keep showering on me, stays with me forever.

Lord Hanuman, Yog Guru Lahiri Mahasaya Ji (Shyama Charan Lahiri), Lord Buddha, Mahavatar Babaji, and other holy- divine souls who enlightened the path through visions, dreams.

Meenal, my sensei-senpai, for being an awesome friend, spiritual partner, and unconditional support. The most beautiful soul I ever met on earth, who made me understand the true meaning of universal Love and the first unofficial and gratis editor of the book. Gratitude falls short for the countless things, especially, for trusting me enough to go ahead on this route and attempt writing a book in the first place. One in whom patience and wisdom of the hills and flow of the river courses abound.

Neil Kad, my high-spirited nephew, for being the absolute worst and most annoying person I know (You're right to say it about me as well!) and one of the sweetest as well. Additionally, for being a technical mentor and helping me lay out the website and develop various other technical things too. He can be reached at www.elcodigocompany.com

Mr Sunil, for being the first inspiration behind this journey. All those childhood spiritual conversations at our favourite food joint have actually been the foundation of my growth. Without your love, care and support this would never have been possible. Thank you for always understanding me, never judging me, letting me having those experiences, accepting all the craziness with an open heart and being that strong pillar of my life.

Thank you for loving me like a parent, and guiding me like a friend, unconditionally, not just for the book, but for many things about life and what not. Family is not just the people with whom you are born and live, but those as well who are a family to your soul, who become your family by filling your core. You are the one!

Mrs Renu, words may fall short for all your love, warmth, care, and support in many ways. My safe abode. Thank you so much for dedicating most of your life for my wellbeing and concern.

Heru, my biggest critic, and my protector in so many ways. All the experiences I had with you strived me to be a better version of my own self. Your wisdom, knowledge and awareness helped me in so many ways in this spiritual journey. I cannot thank you enough for everything you have gone through for me.

Hemant, for all the little things and the big things. Gratitude for always supporting me and giving me space to be me as me. For trying to accept and trust with an open mind all the versions I have experienced in this journey. For being my best friend and companion, for being you as you.

Robin Mol, for being a wonderful spiritual friend. For your unconditional help whenever it was needed the most. For those words of wisdom which pushed to go within and accelerated the journey.

Mansi Chauhan, for being an excellent editor by giving this book more depth and making the conversations more magical and crafty. Stunningly you have dot the i's and cross the t's well.

Shri Sanjay Kumar Tiwari, for being not just a fantastic co-worker, but also an excellent friend and a guide. Our spiritual conversations over a cup of tea or while walking on the roof of our office building in the lunch break shall always be close to my heart.

Kevin (Pseudonym), for being an amazing human that you are, a wonderful Co Ordinator, and the ease you brought on the table for connecting with the publisher and getting things done so smoothly.

Pranavi Jha, for being such a nice Publication Manager. Repentance for being obnoxiously after you to meet the deadlines to make this book a reality.

To the cover designers and illustrators - **Muskan Sachdeva and Pooja Bishnoi**, for making this book much more beautiful and artful. Gratitude for the patience!

Rajat Arora, for being a lovely and lively brother and a constant encouragement always. Also, to help with some inputs and connecting with some lovely people as well as technology.

My parents, for providing the family support and foundation. Mom has been the one who introduced me to the world of literature first hand and always supported in reading and writing different cults since childhood. Also, for flooding me with the ideas for marketing the book (Inscrutable at times as well!).

Soniya and Akanksha for being super excited about the book, always.

Big Cheers to all the readers, seekers, around the world.

Lastly, to each and every soul who crossed my path, either giving me a learning/ lesson or much needed support and love.

~~~ May every soul in distress, be bestowed with one Gauri and Tanmay! ~~~

www.ingramcontent.com/pod-product-compliance
Lightning Source LLC
LaVergne TN
LVHW041700060526
838201LV00043B/504